Reviews of The Bucks

'At last a genuinely funny book about the City and the rise and fall of the roaring eighties, written by a brutally sacked equity salesman. Opening in Year Zero of the depression – 1990 – the first five pages put the boot into one Capital City myth after another; the dealing room at UBS Phillips and Drew resembles an airport terminal, the firm manages to poach only differs from other brokers, and the presence of P&D pundits on TV programmes was a "sure sign of mediocrity".

And as for the author's estimates of his own talents: "My boss … thought I was 'crap'… he had managed to spot the one thing that I hoped would go unremarked." This could be the City's version of Final Cut. Buy, buy, buy.'

Dan Atkinson
The Guardian, 4th July 1994

'Parton is very good at explaining City technicalities – headhunters, insider trading, the uses or otherwise of stock-analytical advice – in a clear, chatty, down-to-earth read.'

Jenny Turner
The Guardian, 19th July 1994

' "I couldn't see the point of suffering in the City of London if the sums I earned were only mildly revolting as opposed to completely obscene." It's the kind of opening that hints at plenty of juice to come; Parton delivers on the promise.

There's always the fear with this kind of book – self-confessed hopeless stockbroker bares soul and puts boot into former employers—that embarrassment or failure to amuse lurks over the very next page. Relax. Parton avoids those sins. He has written a very funny book, required reading for all the forlorn City saps who are still playing the game.

Parton kicks off with him married to a Japanese television workaholic, five years into a City broking life, employed by UBS Phillips and Drew. His facility with the Japanese language and a modicum of chutzpah has persuaded successive ignorant City firms that he will one day land them a tidal wave of Japanese cash, as eager Tokyo investors suddenly discover European equities.

What goes up – Parton freely admits he was never good enough to go very far up – must come down. He nosedives into unemployment and, yes, does discover an alternate life, playing the piano, writing, enjoying himself without loads of dosh.

That might sound twee. But buckets of black humour, ready side-swipes at City taboos – including this newspaper – suffocate sentimentality on sight. It's just too funny, even when things turn sombre; for instance, when Parton's wife dumps him and walks of with their child.

Everyone deservedly gets a going-over: broking firms; headhunters – Parton calls them all "Donald" since they are individually indistinguishable; even the 'colleague' who told him Parton that he would not speak to him if he wore a checked shirt to the office. So, for the price of an upmarket City sandwich you can buy an afternoon's wonderful hilarity, far funnier and less pompous than *Liar's Poker*.'

Gary Mead
Financial Times, 4th July 1994

'One of this year's funniest reads. Hilarious.'

Margarette Driscoll
The Sunday Times, 17th July 1994

The Bucks Stop Here

Jim Parton

HARRIMAN HOUSE LTD

3A Penns Road
Petersfield
Hampshire
GU32 2EW
GREAT BRITAIN

Tel: +44 (0)1730 233870
Fax: +44 (0)1730 233880
Email: enquiries@harriman-house.com
Website: www.harriman-house.com

Published in Great Britain in 2009 by Harriman House
Copyright © Jim Parton

The rights of Jim Parton to be identified as the author have been asserted in
accordance with the Copyright, Design and Patents Act 1988.

ISBN 978-1-905641-00-0

British Library Cataloguing in Publication Data
A CIP catalogue record for this book can be obtained from the British Library

Printed in the UK by the MPG Books Group.

About The Author

Born in Nairobi in 1959, Jim Parton was educated at Haileybury and St Andrews University, where he read French (but only for the two weeks before finals). After a short career in the City, he has become a freelance writer. For some years he ran the charity Families Need Fathers. His books include *Unreasonable Behaviour*, *Let Me Entertain You* (for Robbie Williams) and *Walking on Air* (for Trevor Jones). He is married, with four small children, the oldest of whom is four. He and his wife live in Silesian Poland where they are restoring a former bishop's palace.

1

I couldn't see the point of suffering in the City of London if the sums I earned were only mildly revolting as opposed to completely obscene. It was make or break; either up or out. I'd been a stockbroker for five years and I really wasn't rich enough. I was doing well at UBS Phillips and Drew, a respectable, if crumby, firm but not well enough.

It seemed to me that there was a window of opportunity that led into the financial stratosphere, but it would soon be closed. My clients were Japanese investment institutions which had just poured trillions of Yen into European stock markets, optimistic that the unification of Germany and 1992 would lead to a new economic miracle. I thought I would be able to trade myself up because a lot of broking firms saw these trillions as just the start of the arrival of a Wall of Money from Japan.

The Japanese had had loads of money to spare after twenty years of raking it in from the rise and rise in their stock and property markets. In early 1990, however, the Nikkei had collapsed, and it seemed to me that property would not be far behind. The domino effect would soon hit other asset markets strongly influenced by the Japanese. The evidence was there for all to see in the plummeting values of second-hand Van Goghs, Ferraris, golf course developments in Esher and condominiums in Hawaii. Second-hand Jim Partons would be next. I was a 'sell', and had to put myself on the market immediately.

A broker in my position, sensing that he could squeeze more money out of a situation, would normally stride into the boss's office and threaten to leave if his pay were not upped immediately. The trouble is that in my case they would probably have said 'Fine Jim, go'. I had an enemy in Tokyo; he was doing very nicely out there on a tax-free salary and saw me as a threat, because I could speak Japanese and he couldn't. It would have made sense for us to swap jobs. He was senior to me and made sure it didn't happen by sending hostile faxes to my boss every so often about my ineffectualness. He had a point; I was a lousy broker, but such details have rarely been known to hold back a career at Phillips and Drew, so I felt quite hard done by.

With the road to riches at P & D blocked, I was more than amenable to a discreet suggestion from an acquaintance at Merrill Lynch that I should consider an interview to work there.

I had been at Phillips and Drew for almost two years, a long time by recent City standards. It was an extraordinary firm. With a reputation for being bland even before the Union Bank of Switzerland had bought it, it was amorphous, inchoate, a vast blob of ectoplasm absorbing and suffocating all the young men and the handful of women in its path. The dealing room, equal largest in the City with the UBS bond floor downstairs, had all the excitement of Heathrow Terminal Four. We sat in six or seven forty-yard rows of salesmen, analysts and dealers. Stockbroking by the Henry Ford method: you could have any colour you wanted, provided that it was grey. Even the corporate Swatches I gave to my clients at Christmas were grey.

As a financial institution, P & D's chief merit is that it is enormous. If you want to find out about almost any company in Europe, somebody there will be able to tell you. It is unlikely that the analyst will be full of analysis, but he will at least have a set of earnings forecasts and a competent understanding of the crucial financial ratios.

P & D pundits are often interviewed on telly, and quoted in the papers, a sure sign of mediocrity. When I was at Citicorp Scrimgeour Vickers, in its period of steepest decline, its analysts started to appear with great frequency in the market reports of the *Financial Times*. If Scrimgeour had actually been doing the business, it would have been the last place they would want to have appeared; the client would be furious at the indiscretion. I didn't have to trawl through many copies of the *FT* to find this example: 'British Steel edged ahead 11/2p to 681/2p after its broker, UBS Phillips and Drew, turned buyer of the shares.' Sixty salesmen, on a day the market rose 26 points to 2,516, could only push a major house stock up 11/2p.

There was absolutely no way that P & D made UBS any money. With my computer system, flashing telephone board, floor space, company car and share of deal settlement, I must have cost them at least £250,000 a year to employ, of which salary was only £35,000. Multiply that by 300, add in the cost of all the hospitality suites upstairs, plus the salaries of half a dozen burghers of Zurich called Ruedi, and you got some pretty big numbers.

Take a look at commission income from a typical salesman such as me, and you got some pretty small numbers.

Logically, UBS should have closed P & D down, although it would have been an expensive process, entailing the loss of a large amount of face back in Zurich, not to mention London. But there may be entirely different reasons as to why it has been kept going. Who knows? Certainly not I.

There is a rule in Switzerland that deposits unclaimed after fifty years belong to the bank that holds them. About that length of time ago rather a lot of wealthy middle Europeans lost their lives unexpectedly. Many of them would have put their money in numbered Swiss bank accounts for safety. In the 1990s, many Swiss banks' capital ratios improved substantially, at a time when economic fundamentals suggest they ought to be deteriorating. If such a Swiss bank had a subsidiary that loses lots of money, this process could be made to look a lot less embarrassing.

Swiss bureaucracy had taken hold at P & D and management was chaotic. I used to reckon that if I were to stop phoning clients altogether, it would be at least three months before anyone noticed. I put something close to this theory to the test; not on purpose, but because I felt unenthusiastic about my job, and unenthusiastic about what the analysts were telling me to tell my clients, whom I therefore didn't call all that often.

There were frequent changes and the creation of new responsibilities. A new memo would arrive on my desk each day along the lines of: 'Smith will spearhead the marketing of Belgian equities into Andorra. Smith's duties will be taken over by Jones, our new hiring from Warburgs.' If Jones was leaving Warburgs it was because he was not a particularly high flier, and had realised that UBS was the only firm in the City still coughing up inordinate sums for his ilk. Which made it very ironic that I would need to leave P & D to earn my fortune.

The head of equities at P & D was Hector Sants, who despite being no older than most of his staff, was a somewhat remote figure. It was usually his signature on the memos about Belgian equities.

One should not despise mediocrity, as the purveyance thereof undoubtedly fills a market niche; a lot of fund managers don't like razor-sharp stockbrokers because they feel intimidated by them. It is comforting to be brighter than your broker, which is perhaps why people with first class degrees almost never make good salesmen.

Also, if you understand too much about what you are saying, you spot the contradictions and find it difficult to continue. Sadly I can't use a first as an explanation for my failure as a salesman.

My boss Jonathan didn't either.

I regarded him as a thick, ignorant, abrasive, card-carrying nasty bastard. He didn't have a degree, but he did have see-the-wood-for the-trees intelligence, a capacity to explain things very clearly, to see the big picture. He was one of the most successful salesmen P & D had and had thus been promoted to manager. He couldn't manage much, but he did manage to spot the one thing that I had hoped would go unremarked. He said he thought I was 'crap'.

There was one black person on the entire UBS trading floor. Of course, occasionally a black person would come and fix your computer, and you'd see plenty of Somali cleaners if you were working late at night, but Sharon was different. She worked on the economics team and fancied transferring to sales.

I bumped into her on the Northern Line going home one evening where she explained that she'd asked Jonathan whether she could join our team, and he'd said 'No'.

'He was very honest about it,' she said without rancour. 'He said he knew it was wrong, but he couldn't help himself, he didn't want a woman on his team. I respect him for being so upfront about it.'

I'd heard a different explanation from Jonathan. To me he'd said, 'Sharon, she's quite good, but I could never have her on my team. She's black.'

I think it unlikely that P & D would have fired me, but it was clear that I was unlikely to get richer there, either through an increase in my salary, or a rise into management, where I could begin to assist in the setting of my bonus. I rang up and accepted the Merrill Lynch interview offer.

When I went to see my future boss, Alick, at Merrill's, it was clear that he had more or less made up his mind to offer me a job. He'd had this brilliantly original idea that stock sold by British and American clients could be bought by the Japanese, and vice versa, thus improving his distributive power. The only doubt in his mind was whether I would accept their offer. I was, after all, fluent in Japanese with five years' broking experience, so presumably I could pick and choose.

The first interview therefore went swimmingly and I was called in for another to meet the 'rest of the team'. This meeting took place over a few pints in a pub with Alick and his two colleagues Henry and Charlie, the latter of whom eschewed pints in favour of rather effete bottles of tasteless Mexican lager with lime sticking out of the top. I said I liked the idea of working in a team of four as opposed to the fifty or so at P & D, but made sure that they understood that Japanese money earmarked for overseas was still mainly tied up in Tokyo, so they shouldn't expect too much of me in London. They assured me that they understood, and took a long-term view.

So far in the interview process I had been protected from senior management. After the pub I was taken in to meet Michael Hewitt. Mike Hewitt! I was at school with him. He was a year below me and a prize prat as far as I could recall. He had been an unusual teenage rebel. Back in 1977-ish, he wore the broadest bell-bottoms with which he could get away without expulsion, but unlike most teenage rebels his hair, jacket, indeed the bell-bottoms themselves were immaculate. He used to glide, ineffably smooth on highly polished illegal cowboy boots, with ridiculously impractical, forward sloping heels.

Thirteen years later the hair was still like the Virgin's Conception, but bell-bottoms had given way to another form of rebellion, this time against City pinstripe. I am all for rebellions against the City dress code, which seems bent on making everyone look like Alan Sugar, but I found Mike's olive-green suit from Milan with brown Guccis a bit disconcerting.

It was not entirely clear what his role was – he was in management – but he filled me in on Merrill Lynch and its ethos. He went on and on, seamlessly, and I soon lost track. They had something called matrix management. Mike was as smooth as he had been at school and had clearly mastered matrix management, or at least talking about it, which is the key in these things. He could even manage the plural of matrix correctly.

The three pints I had had were beginning to percolate through my system and I wished he would hurry up.

Mike clearly had me confused with an older, brainier brother who used to win the Pratt Latin unseen prize and the Smedley-Turgess Greek poetry prize every year by being the only person in the school to go in for them. As he went up for his tenth academic prize one Speech Day somebody could be heard from a few rows back saying, 'My God, is that Pongo Parton's son – he must have married somebody clever.' Sadly I had inherited my father's brains not my mother's. A similar thing must have happened in the Hewitt family, because he recommended to Alick that I should be hired.

I had also inherited my father's bladder – my entire family suffer from a high metabolic rate combined with low capacity, necessitating visits to the loo at short intervals.

Final hurdle. I met the Americans. Along with other US firms like Salomon Brothers or Morgan Stanley, Merrill Lynch has the reputation of being lean, mean, keen, thrusting, determined, ruthless, tenacious, assertive, sharp, not to say aggressive, so I was on my guard, but this interview was also a pushover. I had a pleasant chat with a nice grandfatherly man who was in charge of sales, and a nice, short, rotund, grandmotherly lady from the Bronx who was in charge of research. She was clearly clueless – who am I to criticise? – but had a misshapen sort of charm. I noticed a rather intriguing little gold anklet under her stocking dating presumably from svelter, sexier days.

After all these meetings I just had time for a further brief meeting with Alick who was thinking in terms of £45,000 a year. My bladder was killing me by this stage, so I just said 'I'll think about it, goodbye,' and then dashed back to P & D.

In the evening I was phoned at home.

'£55,000,' said Alick tentatively.

We settled on sixty. I promised I would try to persuade P & D to reduce the three-month notice period I was on.

As I handed in my letter of resignation the next day, the head of overseas equities said 'Jim, I think you've made absolutely the right decision,' which was definitely not in the script. When a high-flier resigns, he is supposed to be kept 'out of the market' so that the firm he is leaving can nick his clients. I'd been thinking of three months of paid leisure on a yacht in the Mediterranean. 'I expect you'll want to start as soon as possible so we'll reduce your notice period to a month. You can leave immediately.'

I visited Merrill Lynch towards lunchtime.

'How did it go?' asked Alick. 'Did you have trouble persuading them to let you leave?'

'Yes,' I replied. 'But they gave up when they realised how determined I was.'

2

For my month's notice period, I booked a flight to Egypt with Gen, my three-year-old son. This is pronounced with a hard 'g' as in Ghengis, not 'Jen'. People always ask what it means, and it's nothing to do with the great Khan. It means 'origin' or 'fountainhead', which may sound silly, but it was chosen by both sets of grandparents, largely because it is easy to pronounce.

My wife Rika couldn't come because of the pressure of work. She helps Japanese TV companies when they come across to make documentaries, and when she is busy, she is very busy.

In Cairo I stayed with an old university friend called Andrew, who had done a Cat Stevens. I had to come to terms with calling him Osman, and being greeted by a bearded kiss on both cheeks, and Gen had to be dissuaded from jumping on Osman's back when he prostrated himself at odd times of the day, but Andrew didn't mind, and was delighted with Gen's wailing impression of the Islamic call to prayer. Overall we had a tremendous time. Gen shouted his head off inside Tutankhamun's tomb and inside the Great Pyramid of Cheops, where, being only three foot tall, he could charge up the tunnel inside while I was on my hands and knees. He might also be the youngest person ever to have visited the top of one of the great pyramids illegally (the small one on the left of the Benson and Hedges advert, jolly big when you get up it). The only hazardous moment came when we got lost in a Nubian village on Elephant Island in Aswan, trying to find a shortcut to the five star hotel to watch England vs West Germany on the lobby telly.

A friendly young man in flowing robes approached me, and seeing Gen perched on my arm, pointed at some mangos in a tree.

'Third World interacts with First World in harmony,' I thought. 'We are going to have a beautiful experience.' When he had got me round the corner he leant on my shoulder and gave me an enormous kiss. 'When in Nubia, do as the Nubians,' was not my first reaction, but although disconcerted, I remained polite. To make his meaning less ambiguous the young man then attempted to mount my leg, like an untrained male Labrador excited by the sudden arrival of, say, Joan Collins.

I didn't stay to discover where the mangos fitted into the man's imagination. Gen and I made it to the hotel where we settled down with a group of bricklayers from Hackney to watch the match. West Germany beat England on penalties. Gen was not as concerned with Chris Waddle missing the net as he should have been. He kept asking in a loud voice, 'Daddy, why did the man in the nightie kiss you?'

I had a one-day attack of the Pharaoh's Revenge, but Gen was fed for the sake of his health on Fanta, bananas, peanuts and crisps and was fit throughout. He has been asking to go back ever since.

I started at Merrill Lynch in the middle of July.

Two weeks later, on August 2nd, 1990, Saddam Hussein invaded Kuwait.

3

A huge wave of relief might have been expected to sweep the financial markets with the Gulf War ceasefire. Instead it was the signal for a return to stock market torpor. The start of the war had got people frantically dealing, so the end proved to be an anti-climax. It was already too late to buy.

The grim reaper moved away from the Iraqi slit trenches and visited the equities trading floor at Merrill Lynch, where a market maker, a salesman and the two most attractive girls in the office were made redundant.

The salesman was delighted because he had taken out redundancy insurance, which for surprisingly modest premiums would pay him more than he had been earning anyway for two years. In his spare time he had been contributing to the Jewish hour on Spectrum radio, and he could now pursue his ambition to build a career as a disc jockey. His name isn't yet sufficiently well known to drop, but I have seen him a couple of times on Sky Super Channel. (Just in case he gets famous I mention that he has changed his name from Mark Jaffé to Mark Jeffries.) The thought crossed my mind that I should investigate this insurance.

The girls were tearful and, being 'foolish virgins', had no insurance. They were going to be a great loss to sexist bastards like myself who enjoyed looking them up and down but apart from the intangible economic benefit of keeping morale high with male staff (the overwhelming majority in any City office), they were an obvious area for cost cutting.

The market maker, Ron, trying to look brave and not unmanned, was ashen-faced.

'You'll get another job with your experience, Ron.'

'It's not the environment, Jim, but I'll be all right.'

Since the 1987 Crash, mass redundancy had been a feature of City life, but virtually everyone who lost his job soon found another, frequently better paid. I feared that for solid, competent, but unexceptional people like Ron, such times were running out.

On the other hand I was slightly envious, having had no holiday in the eight months since joining Merrill Lynch. Egypt was a distant, fond memory. A skiing holiday was coming up soon but a decent spell of redundancy would not go amiss, if healthily paid for by the Prudential. Insuring myself would be prudent; my Japanese clients had been decidedly quiet thanks to Saddam Hussein and although I was in constant receipt of assurances that Merrill Lynch were Here-For-The-Long-Term, the place had the feel of Bomber Command circa 1943. There was a pervasive if forced jollity as people failed to come back from sorties into the boss's office. At the back of most people's minds was the thought, 'Ron bought it in the last lot, who's next?'

Despite the change of firm, I still didn't like stockbroking. I was like a Norwegian Blue pining for the fjords. From where I sat it was impossible to tell whether it was a sunny day outside the airless office in which I squandered my disappearing youth, but much as I'd have liked to have been doing something completely different, I was in a trap. My mortgage was larger than the value of my house in fashionable Camberwell, I had a free-spending wife, a fearsome Japanese of Korean descent, and four-year-old Gen due to go to an income absorbing school soon, plus an overdraft that seemed to grow in direct proportion to the amount of money I was earning. This last, a not inconsiderable amount, was scarcely stratospheric by City standards, even if it was more than the Chancellor of the Exchequer.

I glanced at my Reuters screen in an attempt to piece together clues as to which way the dollar might be going, and what effect that would have on European company profits. It didn't take long to decide that I didn't care.

At times like this, when the stock markets were quiet, which despite the popular image was almost all of the time, I would ring up a tame client called Mr Hoshide. I had no sensible advice to offer him, and he had only a tiny fund. The importance of the relationship lay in the fact that we could engage each other ad nauseam in inane conversations about interest rates, or interim results, thereby looking busy and professional to our respective colleagues. I could speak Japanese to him, and thus appear to be working when in fact we might be discussing sumo or rugby. If I called him five times it would look as if I had called five clients.

Mr Hoshide worked in the tiny London investment office of a giant life assurance company. A charming and amusing man, he had the faults at times of being a bit over meticulous, and pedantic, but at heart was a long way from the stereotypical Japanese, being comfortingly idle.

The stereotype is in any case wrong. Idleness is a trait you find in more and more Japanese, particularly of thirty or under. Office workers put in fabulous hours, but they don't work hard. Japan is beginning to suffer from advanced country disease, with a real option on leaving school of decadence rather than work.

The Japanese people suffered during the war, then suffered building the world's mightiest economy. The parents and grandparents of the current generation of young adults don't want to put their children through what they went through. People like Mr Hoshide were thus thoroughly spoilt and pampered as kids. So was my wife.

Mr Hoshide was on a two-year stint in London. He was thrilled to be away from the one-and-a-half-hour each way commute he had in Tokyo and the long, long hours in the office, a lot of them spent reading cartoon books to pass the time, followed by the duty of going out to get pissed with workmates. Mrs Hoshide liked London because she didn't have to put him to bed drunk so often, then kick him out of bed at 7 a.m., still stinking.

As a salesman, the best use I could be to him was to supply easily reworkable reports from our analysts that he could send back to his head office, passing them off as his own work.

Most evenings I followed a complex routine of picking up Gen from his friend Rory's nanny, whipping round Tesco, then processing him for bed, my wife usually being busy until late with her Japanese TV people. Normally I would have to read half a dozen Thomas the Tank Engine stories, but that night, with the Gulf ceasefire just announced, Gen and I opted to watch the Nine O'Clock News in the parental bedroom; he loved all the burnt-out tanks and lorries and the sand reminded him of Egypt.

'When can I go to Egypt and have Coca Cola and crips (sic) again?' he asked.

Eight o'clock was his putative bed time, but not a target ever attained.

I have no recollection of the end of the news, only of being shaken awake by my affectionate wife, Rika, with a requirement to expel Gen back to his quarters. The television was still on. I attempted to cling to consciousness for a little while in the vain hope of getting lucky, but the telephone went. Knowing it would be a Japanese colleague freshly unsqueezed from his morning train with an earnest desire to talk cathode ray tubes, I went to sleep.

Friday's morning meeting would normally have been greeted with more enthusiasm than most. In this one, however, the news was that German truck sales were weakening, the dollar was basing, and East Germans were going on strike. Dullsburg, Schleswig-Holstein.

I battled manfully to stave off sleep as half a dozen stock analysts talked us through their ideas of the day by taking frantic notes. Later I rang up my Japanese clients and bored them rigid with what I had heard. Unsurprisingly I received no orders that day.

Talking to the Japanese is an activity that requires specialists at the best of times, because their English is so dire, and because of a prejudice exacerbated by the likes of Clive James that they have no sense of humour and are just a tiny little bit mad. Madness cannot be held against them, after all, the British are palpably a little bit mad too, and in my opinion a degree of madness is healthy. Imagine how awful it would be to be Swiss.

The perception that the Japanese have no sense of humour is wrong. These days even Clive James laughs with them rather than at them, the sneer replaced by something approaching affection. Humour is language based and sadly a lot gets lost in translation, so proving my thesis that the Japanese can be witty is tricky, but take it from me, it's not unknown. Having said that, Japanese fund managers are as dull as English fund managers.

My job was made doubly difficult by the mess their financial institutions had got themselves into in believing that their stock and property markets would rise forever. Despite falling by a third, Tokyo's stock market continued to look very expensive by Western standards, and anomalies remained, such as the grounds of the Emperor's Palace continuing to be worth more than the state of California. Should anybody undo the bits of string and sticky tape holding the whole thing together, the collapse would be spectacular. Preventing this was where Japanese financial firepower was concentrated, so there was little spare cash for investing overseas and enriching the likes of me.

I assumed that my employers did not understand this. After all, they had taken me on a mere eight months previously when such things should have been pretty obvious. Very intelligent people rarely get to the top in stockbroking because they offend too many stupid people on the way up, and end up being stabbed in the back. This could be true of any profession – politics springs to mind. Our managers at Merrill's were all Americans in their fifties who had got to where they were by offending nobody.

The grandfatherly head of sales, and the grandmotherly head of research, had told me when I arrived that it would not be too long before the Japanese became a force to be reckoned with in European equities. Their experience of the Japanese and of European equities was garnered selling US equities to American private investors for thirty years in Peoria, Pa. I hoped that they would keep thinking bullishly about Japan a little longer, because my secret personal view was pretty cataclysmic. The Japanese were in such shit that it would be perhaps five years before levels of activity made a decent recovery, but with luck it would be a couple of years before Merrill

Lynch realised this, so that I could continue to earn more than the Chancellor for producing next to nothing. Merrills would continue to travel hopefully rather than arrive. By the time they realised that with me they would never arrive, I would be on my way to yet another new firm.

Selling on hope had been a speciality of mine. I speak fluent Japanese, therefore it was assumed that I would be able to communicate very efficiently with Japanese investors and persuade them to do their investment through me. In five years I had worked for five companies. The first three, Laurence Prust, Vickers da Costa, and Scrimgeour Vickers, have all been closed down by the foreign banks who bought them. I was the eternal trainee, always promising lots, but in terms of revenues delivering nothing. Each time I came under pressure to produce, I changed jobs – switching from selling UK equities to the Japanese to selling Japanese equities to the UK, then back again to selling UK equities to the Japanese, then finally Europe to the Japanese. I was well into my third year as a stockbroker before getting my first order, yet my salary nearly doubled each of those years.

I started on £11,000 at Laurence Prust, and left them eight months later for £17,000 at Vickers da Costa, which became part of Citicorp Scrimgeour Vickers. Almost exactly a year later there was a massive storm in London. I cycled to work, ducking the fallen trees, and was one of the few to make it in. My boss was one of the others. I had announced my intention of transferring internally from the Vickers da Costa bit, where I was a trainee Japanese equity salesman, to become a trainee UK equities salesman in the Scrimgeour Kemp Gee bit, selling to the Japanese. My idea was that I would be one of few Brits able to talk to his clients in their native language. The Wall of Money was coming.

My boss tried to dissuade me. He pointed out that commission rates were lower in the UK. I hadn't quite worked out the direct link between commission earned on the one hand, and salary and bonus received on the other. These things were just paid to me, without my understanding why. With the benefit of hindsight, I can see that my failing to spot this crucial relationship was responsible for my failure to become obscenely rich. If only I'd stuck with Japanese equities, or better still, gone into Japanese warrants.

My boss gave me a £10,000 pay rise. It was Friday 17th October 1987. That afternoon certain perturbations began to occur over on Wall Street, and by Monday, markets worldwide were in free fall. I still made the transfer to Scrimgeours, but they paid £10,000 more for me than they would have.

At this stage, I had never had an order as such. I had offered stock once.

'Where is it?' I was asked. This had seemed a funny question at the time. Why did the fund manager care where it was? The back office would cope with that. 'Locked up in some bank vault somewhere, I suppose,' I answered.

'No, where is it?'

'I don't know, I'll go and ask someone,' I volunteered helpfully, and leant across to ask a colleague, who informed me that 'where', in City parlance means 'how much'.

At this stage in my career, having never received an order, and not understanding that 'where' can mean 'how much', I was worth £27,000 a year to my employer. By the time I had three years on my C.V. it was a bit difficult to disguise the fact that I might actually have accumulated some experience, so rather than promising what I myself would become, I promised what my client base would become. The Japanese had scarcely diversified a fraction of their mammoth portfolios into Europe, as so far it had all gone to the US, but the great Wall of Money was confidently predicted. The terrific thing about the Wall of Money was that nobody knew when it would arrive. You had to be prepared, because by the time it did arrive the Japanese, with their notorious love of long-term relationships, would only give business to the brokers who they knew and trusted. Therefore you had to employ Jim Parton. The consequences of missing this bonanza were too terrible to contemplate, so even if for the moment I produced little in the way of commission, a great day would come, it was imagined, when I and my team would support the rest of whatever firm I worked for.

So far, of course, the Wall of Money had never arrived and to me at least it was obvious that it never would, but I felt pretty safe. Management at Merrill Lynch was as chaotic as at P & D. Since my arrival, Mike Hewitt, plus the nice grandfatherly head of sales, who had been my direct boss, and the rotund granny from the Bronx with the sexy anklet, had all gone on to different things and whilst Merrill Lynch New York or Tokyo might have sound views on Japan's economy available for dissemination, inter-office rivalry would prevent them ever reaching my new boss's ears and poisoning his view of my long-term worth to London.

However, the new boss was at least twenty-five years younger than the grandfatherly head of sales, and keen to make his mark, so I would have to be on my guard.

Chopping non revenue earners is an easy way of demonstrating corporate machismo, even if it is at the expense of the long term.

Keep a low profile, draw that fat salary and survive was my philosophy. A Little, Oscillating Dick, as opposed to a Big Swinging one.

4

At the end of the week it was amazing how tired I'd get, given how little I had actually exerted myself. All stockbrokers believe they do a hard, stressful job and therefore justify the pay they earn. There is no doubt that a certain amount of discipline is required, to get in at 7.45 and survive until 5.30, and read the *FT*, which would be the world's dullest newspaper if the *Wall Street Journal* were not duller. But it doesn't take long to read the three articles a day in it which are relevant to you. I doubt that more than two per cent of brokers or fund managers ever read the editorial. Meanwhile it costs more than any of the other broadsheets. The *Daily Telegraph* sports section alone gives better value for money.

Some people do work long hours in the City, but usually as a result of some staying-on-at-work competition instigated by those with more ambition than sense. Very few jobs in the City require you ever to have two telephones strapped to the ears à la financial soap, and the infrequent bursts of frenetic activity are interspersed with very long periods of profound tedium, sometimes, no, often, lasting weeks on end.

Stockbrokers do not have stressful lives, and it is easy for incompetent people to avoid being fired. It is sometimes said that we deserve our high pay because we burn out early like soccer stars. This argument is entirely specious. If it is true it is because champagne is bad for you. As for the high pay being compensation for low job security, I fail to identify a correlation between low pay and high security. Somewhat the reverse in fact.

I guess that getting up at 6.30 every day does take its toll, but the only stress generated comes from trying to work up enthusiasm for the machinations of the Bundesbank or the business prospects of some Swedish rock tool manufacturer day in day out. The compensatory buzz of dealing in huge sums of money and calculating the percentage that would accrue to my bonus was not one that I often had.

Weekends were spent recovering from the Bundesbank or the rock tool manufacturer. It's a shame to waste one's precious days off, but usually I achieved nothing beyond a bit of shopping. Rika would give me inviolable instructions to dust mantelpieces, change sheets, wash them, hoover upstairs, put the rubbish out, clean the stove, buy some new shoes for Gen and other exciting leisure time activities. I violated them, I rebelled, I did nothing.

On Sundays, if nothing had been organised, Gen and I would nip round the corner to the local car boot sale to marvel at the array of merchandise on offer; most of which would be thrown away by Oxfam. I always came back at least a fiver poorer to the despair of Rika, who had a tendency to be less optimistic about the investment potential of my restoration projects.

With the junk we bought, Gen could recreate the road to Basra on News at Ten or, by the imaginative removal of tyres from toy cars and juxtaposition of Lego, an authentic Camberwell street scene. The fact that he possessed only broken toys made trips to his friend Rory's house, with all its expensive kit from the Early Learning Centre, all the more exciting for him. Rory was a poisonous child, but because our toys didn't come up to scratch we rarely had to reciprocate hospitality. This isn't quite fair. Rory very much liked Gen's broken toys, but Rory's parents, being pushy, wanted him to Learn things Early. It really is a very clever name for a toy shop. You can't help wishing a child with dyslexia on parents like Rory's. They were also very keen for Rory to grow up as liberal on the subject of race as they were. Gen, being of yellowish hue, was a gentle initiation before exposure to the really hard stuff.

The tyranny of the Sunday papers was one of the worst things about being a stockbroker. It was dismal to have to plough through all that dreary journalism on company results and contracts on one's day off on the vague chance that a journalist had come up with something that we didn't know or fabricate a week ago.

I cycled in to work. In the world of the company GTI this marked me out as eccentric, but I did it because it was the only regular exercise I got, and public transport was so hopeless, and even on my wages I baulked at the cost of parking in the City. My colleagues Charlie and Henry shared a car in from near Camberwell, but that meant getting to Charlie's house by 7 a.m. which was about half an hour too early for me, (or two and a half hours of lost sleep a week).

I kept three suit jackets on the back of my chair and the adjoining trousers in my European equities research filing cabinet, somewhere between Chemicals and Consumer Goods. This was necessary to avoid the tiresome ritual of having them hidden from me each day by Charlie; proof, perhaps, that the British are not necessarily endowed with a more sophisticated sense of humour than the Japanese.

At 7.30 a.m. there were few people about other than my colleagues, mainly ex-Army officers, so rather than walk all the way to the gents I always changed in the middle of the room.

In the morning meeting we learnt that L'Oreal might take over Revlon, that there were some important employment numbers coming up from the United States on Friday, and that Heineken's earnings per share were up, as expected, by 12.3 per cent. Ericsson had won a small order from Kuwait to help rebuild its cellular phone network. And that was it.

Alick, our chief and mentor, ex-Guardsman, Old Etonian, therefore spent the morning writing a militaristic memo to New York demanding that the lazier analysts (nine out of twelve) be sacked. They were in a different league from the analysts at Phillips and Drew in terms of their industry, knowledge and experience, but Alick did have a point that some were lazy. The nice grandmother from the Bronx with the sexy anklet had let them become very "un-American" in their working habits.

To the New York head office, the European equities sales team (only four of us) was just a pimple on the backside of Merrill Lynch, and Alick its suppurating centre, so this memo was unlikely to have more effect than the previous twenty-five.

Meanwhile, Henry, ex-Guardsman, wife's brother went to Eton, went round to the research department to photocopy the *Telegraph* crossword. He had been a more sybaritic, officers' mess kind of soldier than Alick. He definitely hadn't answered a 'Join the Professionals' ad. On days like this he would do about half of the puzzle, then ring up clients and flatter them by asking their advice on the clues he couldn't do. This way of carrying on drove Alick spare, but so long as a large order from one of the flattered clients arrived once a fortnight or so, there was not a great deal he could do about it.

Charlie, very minor public school, Dad in the RAF, straight into the City, children will certainly go to Eton, (if they are bright enough to get in) was at twenty-five the youngest team member. He got directly on to the phone and didn't get off it until he had told all his clients about the Kuwaiti phone order and Heineken's e.p.s., even though all this mundane information was freely available on the Reuters screen. My three colleagues had all come from Swiss Bank Corp, then the Number One in Euro equities, where Charlie had been the most successful of them. His 'This is the News' service was important to fund managers because they needed to know what SBC were up to. The sad fact was that no European fund manager needed to know what Merrill Lynch was doing, so Charlie's commission figures had slipped somewhat. They were still, however, in a different league from mine, but then I was Building-For-The-Long-Term.

(Self: can't quite bring myself to admit minor public school, but it was a shock when I left to discover that most people haven't heard of it. Famous old boy: John McCarthy. I can't remember him at all, although my older brother, a senior prefect, claims to have busted him for smoking.)

Things brightened considerably with the arrival of a new trainee, a lovely Italian girl. She wore a contour-enhancing dress, a sculpted masterpiece of Milanese haute couture, with a zip all the way down the back, which somehow seemed to say, 'undo me'.

She introduced herself. 'I am juicy,' she said. I, and several others, tried not to gasp too visibly.

'You're what?'

'I am juicy,' she repeated, and the truth gradually began to dawn that that was what she wanted to be called. Nobody could quite cope, and variants on Jose and Jessie were tried. It turned out that her name was Giusseppina, or Giussi for short.

Giussi was from the Merrill Lynch MBA training scheme in New York, and therefore knew next to nothing about economics, companies or broking their shares. She would be joining us on sales, but first she was to pick up what she could by observing the work being done by dealers, salesmen and analysts. In due course she would replace a nice, clean-cut young Dane entrusted to us until a few weeks previously, by which time his sincerity and enthusiasm had got us down.

Giussi had a lovely, naïve, doe-eyed way of asking questions, and of perching herself on the end of one's desk in a way that most men, mesmerised, could not resist. 'I am Giussi. Please let me revolve on your desk. I want to learn something,' she'd say to the traders, charmingly oblivious to the double entendre.

Henry and Charlie were soon eating out of her lap, or would have been if they had got half a chance, and even Alick found time away from harassing the American senior management and the research department to help her with her questions.

My Japanese clients remained disquietingly quiet. Alick told me he'd discussed it with his boss, and that it was seventy per cent likely that I would be posted to Tokyo where business was still believed to be brisk (so I told my bosses). Rika would be delighted to be nearer home. I had severe misgivings about twelve-hour working days and proximity to my mother-in-law, although a nice tax free salary through Guernsey would always be welcome.

* * *

The next day I drove to work because it was raining. My Citroen BX 16 valve was not, perhaps, the petrolhead's car of choice, but it went to 135mph and from nought to sixty in 6.9 seconds. A nice little runabout in London. As it was a company car I never cleaned it and the insides had eight months of biscuit and crisp crumbs pressed into the crushed velour of the back seat. In Camberwell there isn't quite the pressure to wash a car that you get in, say, Purley.

I parked it in a very handy parking place just outside the office where the workmen had obliterated the yellow lines.

In the morning meeting we were told that, despite the dramatic pictures of burning oil in Kuwait, the world was awash with the stuff, and its price was likely to weaken for the next six months. Merrill Lynch had predicted a collapse in the oil price almost as soon as Saddam Hussein invaded Kuwait. At the time, the almost universal view was that oil would jump further from forty dollars to sixty or even a hundred, not fall back to twenty dollars as we were saying. It was very pleasing for a salesman to have told his clients something that actually turned out to be true: oil down = inflation down = interest rates down = markets up.

That had been twenty-five per cent ago, and my clients hadn't bought a thing.

The Japanese have a pathological distrust of stockbrokers having been so comprehensively and continuously legged over by the likes of Nomura, so if a broker comes on with a well argued story, inevitably they assume that there must be some sort of catch. In early 1990, the Japanese had been very big buyers of Europe just before the Saddam crash. Because of their losses from this, some had gone as far as to ban their fund managers from investing at all during the war. They made the same mistake during the 1987 crash, thereby missing an opportunity to buy at the bottom.

Xenophobic politicians and protectionists who have complained about the ravages Japanese manufacturers have inflicted on our industry should reflect gratefully for a moment that Japanese investors have always been available to buy at the top, and sell at the bottom of our financial markets, which I suspect redresses the trade imbalance amply. (Not, of course, that the sophisticated and professional British and American fund managers with all their fabulously expensive and complex methods of prediction did any better in the run up to the Gulf War. They were just as scared to buy anything as the 'amateur' Japanese.)

The moral of the story for an investor has been to watch what the Japanese do, and do the opposite, although I am not sure how this investment strategy operates in the new era in which they may have no spare money to invest overseas.

After lunch, Wall Street opened strongly. Somebody from the New York office rang in with the information that there was massive buying of US shares and the largest number of small buy orders for four years. I called some of my clients but couldn't panic them into purchasing anything. I ought to have been telling them to sell, as small orders = private individuals = unsophisticated investors = top of the market. There was no point though: as they hadn't bought at the bottom they could hardly sell at the top.

At the next morning meeting I passed the time doing a survey of Hermès ties. Six out of nine men had them, a not untypical score. Giussi had a Hermès scarf. The three without them were myself, the electronics analyst, making a rare appearance at the meeting to tell us about one of his companies, and an exponent of the dismal science of economics from the bond department. Analysts would compromise their credibility if they dressed fashionably. They need to look gritty and industrial, as if they went to Northern grammar schools. It is always curious to see men on £100,000 a year wearing polyester shirts and ties with gravy stains down them, but it undoubtedly helps clients take them seriously. There must be an Old Etonian ex-Guardsman working as an analyst somewhere in the City, but I have yet to meet him.

By chance I was wearing Armani, bought for me several Christmases ago by Rika in a last ditch attempt to smarten me up, so I felt that I could announce the results of the survey without my own dishevelled appearance being the butt of too many unkind jokes, or being suspected of taking the piss.

This sparked an animated conversation about whether you could get Hermès ties cheaper at JFK, Heathrow or closer to source at Charles de Gaulle; I advocated Hong Kong's excellent forgeries. American employment numbers looming up the very next day no less, temporarily took a back seat, despite the presence of the dismal scientist to explain them to us. Charlie said that he knew a little man who could turn a soiled Hermès tie inside out or back to front or whatever was necessary, and re-stitch it, as new, for as little as thirty-five pounds.

I got three orders, all about £100,000, so it could be said that I was busy. It didn't really compare with the nine million pounds order Henry had been working for Barings over the last few days, or the two million pounds sell order in a defence contractor Alick had been eking out into the market for a Middle Eastern client who was no doubt in a position to make some clever guesses as to who would replace all that hardware lost in the Gulf War. One day the Japanese in London would be BIG in European equities and the market would tremble every time it got wind of an order emanating from Jim Parton. Sadly not yet. Still, Merrill Lynch was there for the long term.

Giussi's father turned out to be the president of the chamber of commerce in Naples. It was only a few days into the job and she got her first order: not bad for a beginner. She hadn't associated the company name – Daimler Benz – with the maker of the upmarket motor cars, but with half a dozen panting men helping her it was soon traded.

It was one of my duties to do the shopping at Tesco having picked up Gen. I liked the Brixton Tesco; they had lots of ethnic food, although Rika still had to travel to a Japanese shop to get the right brands of soy sauce and sesame oil.

As a stockbroker I could keep the shopping process under control, because I was fully conversant with the tricks supermarkets play to improve profits, mainly because in City presentations the heads of Tesco and Sainsbury's boast about them. Tricks like stashing high margin products at the end of the aisles. As you slow to go round them, you see Blanquette de Veau Provençale aux Champignons (Medallions of Tasty Veal in a Savoury Mushroom sauce, Provence style, serves two to four). And because it seems like a good idea at the time, you buy it.

Gen always insisted on driving the trolley, so at the end of most aisles I was usually apologising for a collision, rather than loading up with high margin products. Gen was still not a victim of the great capitalist conspiracy, until, that is, the checkout counter where Tesco cynically stashed all the Crunchies and Smarties, knowing that harassed parents are more likely to give in to their children than cause a scene.

* * *

My skiing holiday was on the way to being arranged, although, as ever, Rika complained that pressure of work would prevent her from going. This was a kind of brinkmanship designed to force the rules of the trip, i.e. I would not abandon her, in a cloud of powder snow, to make her own way down the black piste. I had been skiing since I was six, she since she married me. It was a source of marital tension, made worse by the fact that every year we stayed at my parents' rudimentary ex-ruin, 30km down the valley from Val d'Isere.

As a concession and an incentive, I allowed her to invite Chip, an American friend of hers who had been angling for an invitation.

Alick had been unable to get in a skiing holiday so a few weeks previously I had invited him. It could do no harm to my career, I reasoned, and he was a nice enough chap apart from a certain intolerance: of Henry for doing the crossword, the analysts for doing no work, and of the Americans for being American. His wife was inconsiderately about to drop mewling puker number three, so his skiing plans were up the spout.

Part of the attraction of inviting him was that he said he was a very good skier, and had never skied with anyone better than he, so he might be fun on the slopes. I had also invited Niall, fellow stalwart of the St Andrews University ski team, and completely fearless madman, who used to do scree skiing down disused slag heaps (i.e. with no snow on). I had a lurking fear, or perhaps hope, that Alick would be shown up. And not only by Niall, but by myself, formerly number sixty-three in Great Britain in slalom, and in 1980, the fastest through the bumps at the British Freestyle Championship by six whole seconds (worst points for style, result: second last).

Alick had grown markedly less bullish over the weeks about his brilliant skiing. He hadn't had time to get fit and, because his wife had developed the habit of having a baby at this time of the year, hadn't had a decent skiing holiday for several years. I was gently disabusing him of the notion that he would be staying in my parents' 'chalet', or indeed in a Peter Mayle-style rustic idyll surrounded by lots of cheery yokels with bloodshot cheeks from drinking too much vin rouge. He was going to stay in a converted cowshed, parts of which still contained fossilised cow dung.

5

On Friday evening Rika and I went round to dinner with Rory's parents. Gen and Rory cavorted upstairs until about eleven o'clock. Rory had got Scalectrix for his fifth birthday.

'That's quite a generous present for such a young child,' I remarked to Rory's Dad.

'Oh, it was only ninety-three pounds' he replied. It must have taken considerable negotiation with Rory's Mum to have got away with not getting something wholesome and wooden from the Early Learning Centre for about the same amount of money.

Rory's Mum was adamant that Rory would not be allowed to play with guns, a disappointment to Gen who was heavily into the Gulf War at the time. He became quite adept at smuggling arms into Rory's house. I got a bit of an earful from her about the secret arms factory discovered under Rory's bed. Rory had said Gen made them. I tried to explain that boys play with guns, cars and bicycles, and girls play with dolls, but she would have none of it.

Rory's Dad was a partner in a big City law firm, plutocratic, but slightly embarrassed about it. The other guests were carefully selected to offset capitalist pig-dogs like him and me; a teacher, an artist, a doctor and his wife. Why was it that when asked my profession on occasions like this I always found myself saying 'investment banker' rather than 'equity salesman' or even plain 'stockbroker'?

Next morning, Gen woke up at 8.30-ish, a bit of a result from an exhausted parent's point of view, but still far too early for me. He acceded to my exhortations to go downstairs and play with his toys for about five minutes before coming back up alternatively to bounce on my head and try to force my eyes open with his fingers. For some reason I lost the battle to have a lie-in, so ended up giving the urchin his breakfast while his mother snored on upstairs. In any case, now was the time for sycophancy if I wanted her to come skiing with me; in addition to getting up early I dusted the mantelpieces, changed the sheets, washed them, hoovered upstairs, put the rubbish out, and on Sunday, even bought Gen some boot-legged shoes as instructed (Reebok, five pounds reduced from thirty-five, as smart as Rory's) from the car boot sale.

On Monday I was late to work because, as usual, I had forgotten to iron a shirt. Rika had embraced those parts of the Western feminist canon that suited her with great enthusiasm, and had never been known to do one for me.

My brain was already on holiday. Had it not been, I would have noticed the car pulling out in front of me on the Elephant and Castle roundabout. I had read some reassuring statistics saying that only eighteen Londoners had been killed on bicycles that year, a highly acceptable rate of attrition, making it much safer than the tube. I executed a neat, if involuntary, somersault over the bonnet before landing on my feet unhurt, my bicycle was also undamaged, thereby avoiding becoming the nineteenth. The only casualty was a limp-looking wing mirror on the car.

I recounted my tale to Alick, who said 'I bet he was black'. Irritatingly, he was right.

The morning meeting was dominated by some unpronounceable Swedish company's results; Rock tools good, Cemented Carbide weak, Special Stainless poor, Wire and Strip poor, but Tubes OK, and the tax charge respectably low. Earnings per share would fall in 1991, and probably be lower still in 1992, because of exposure to the US car industry. A bunch of Swedish speculators had been ramping the shares recently so it was an obvious sell. I wondered how I was going to explain all this in Japanese.

Mr Hoshide took the plunge and bought some of the unpronounceable Swedish tool maker; he was humble enough to admit that he had been a bit of a turnip not following my advice on the oil price, and made this order as a sign of trust. £500,000 was a large size for him, indeed the biggest order I'd had for several months. I didn't have the heart to tell him that I had been recommending a sell. Fund managers are grown people and can make their own decisions, I reasoned. Who cared anyway, when the money belonged to a group of policy holders in Fukuoka, a group whose existence was, to me, entirely abstract.

After getting Gen to bed at the unheard of early hour of nine o'clock, I enjoyed a lovely romantic candlelit dinner cooked for me by Rika, who was free, for once, of the exigencies of her jovial Japanese workmates and their requirement to wind down from their documentary on the Changing of the Guard in a karaoke bar.

Over dinner she told me that she would probably be able to come skiing, but on certain conditions.

1. I would carry her skis.
2. Every lunchtime would be spent in a restaurant.
3. I would never abandon her at the top of the mountain and say, 'Meet you by the car'.
4. I would devote time to teaching her how to ski.
5. She would not have to do any cooking, washing or cleaning. (This was not so different from the way things were at home.)
6. On the other hand, she wanted to be in charge of the shopping. (I would use the word 'spending' not 'shopping'.)
7. She demanded a single bed, because she knew what too much vin rouge does to me. (My father, in his concern over the decay in morals coincident with his children's late teens and early twenties, built only bunk beds to a careful design of his own, impossible to push together, but there was still one double bed. I had my hopes.)

Normally, Monday evening would be early-to-bed night, the night when I caught up on the sleep I had failed to catch up on at the weekend, but with a holiday looming I was feeling a bit demob happy, indeed a touch reckless. I had survived a near fatal accident, got some decent business off Mr Hoshide, and the wife was coming skiing. I reckoned I might get luckier still provided, of course, I disabled all Rika's telecommunications equipment so that nobody would ring in from the Tokyo morning to the middle of the English night.

Tuesday morning passed in a haze. I was tired but happy. I didn't even notice what Giussi was wearing.

Mr Hoshide phoned up very excited. His unpronounceable Swedish stock had gone up five per cent already. 'Thank you Parton san, very good recommendation. Why is it so strong today?' I modestly admitted that we'd been doing a bit of buying. The fact that it had been his own stock purchase pushing up the price was neither here nor there. He gave me an order to buy 3,000 Deutsche Bank, another half a million pounds or so. More than adequate recompense for a profitable misunderstanding.

My skiing holiday was virtually arranged, which was just as well with only a few days to go. I always left it to the very last moment in the belief that people would fall over themselves with gratitude at being invited, with the result that by the time it got mentioned to anyone of my choice they had already booked up elsewhere, so I ended up having to invite people like Alick and the wife's friend Chip.

Dramatis Personae, skiing holiday. (Provisional.)

1. Me.
2. Rika (possibly/probably, the latter two-to-one on, favourite).
3. Chip, American friend of above.
4. Niall, lunatic Scotsman.
5. Alick, boss. He would join us in the middle of the first week some time.
6. Verona, twenty-seven, the youngest ever director of Breese, Spotch and Betts, advertising agency.

We were still short of a car, and it occurred to me that Verona probably had a nice company car. A quick telephone call, veiled threat of withdrawal of invitation, and a Maserati Biturbo convertible had been made available, but on condition of Verona bringing her sister Sienna. So,

7. Sienna, younger sister to the above.

Mr Hoshide's Swedish stock went up another seven per cent, making a total of twelve in two days. I advised him to take profits, which he did. I liked Mr Hoshide, he did what he was told. There was a chance he would miss a further rise, but from my point of view to sell was a risk-free recommendation. If he didn't take my advice to take profits, and the stock fell, I would be proved right again. If it went up further he'd pat himself on the back for knowing more about the markets than his broker, so he would be pleased either way.

He told me that he had no plans for the Easter holiday other than to relax, go to the park and do a bit of shopping with his wife. I persuaded him that as he was in Europe for only a short while he should get out and see a bit of it. I even got him to agree to take a couple of extra days off. 'When in Lome, do as the Lomans.' Result: an afternoon on the phone to various travel agents trying to arrange an Easter break for him and Mrs Hoshide.

Since the end of the Gulf War, all those cowards who had been too scared to get on an aeroplane for fear of meeting an untimely death at the hands of Saddam's terrorists had been making up for lost time: as if terrorists would have had any interest at all in nonentities like senior Merrill Lynch management, who were re-emerging from under their stones in New York to take their wives shopping in London and enact some delayed redundancies in London at the same time. They had probably missed the safest travel conditions ever, with all that hysterical extra airport security, and far fewer travellers.

This pent-up demand for travel meant that organising an Easter break for Mr and Mrs Hoshide was next to impossible. Preferred destinations of Venice, Barcelona and Prague being unavailable at the price, I eventually got them on a coach tour of East German industrial installations, topical if nothing else. They would be able to buy themselves a chunk of Berlin Wall, some nice Dresden china to take home, and have themselves photographed next to a Trabbie.

Giussi got some more orders. Her Italian clients were turning out rather well. It all goes to show that it is not what you know, but who you know. What you look like does no harm either.

One excitement at the time was that Alick, Henry and Charlie had been interviewing a Nordic person, who had impressed them a great deal. 'A bit of a bandit,' he had been described as. When asked his salary, he had named successively higher figures to each of them, as he felt more confident.

Logistically, I wondered how this was going to work, because there weren't any spare work stations in our area.

Nordic people are staid and dull on paper, but they can out-spiv any East Ender. Scandinavian institutions, out of naïvety one assumes, are used to paying far larger commissions on international stocks than others. You can often make them pay 0.5 per cent commission on a UK stock, for example, when a UK institution might pay 0.2 per cent or nothing at all.

I had an exciting time picking up Gen from Rory's. I double-parked, as usual, leaving the keys in the ignition, as usual. When Gen and I turned to walk to where the car had been, only ten yards from the house, it had gone. Nicked, purloined, schnaffeled, rustled, Rikappropriated. I had had my back turned to it for a maximum of a minute. Rory's Mum saw a man take it as she was talking to me.

'Oh, I didn't realise it was yours.' Her description for the police was particularly useful. 'Man in a green sweatshirt.'

I dialled 999 for the first time in my life.

'Police, fire or ambulance?'

'Police, quick.' Three minute wait.

Any chance of heading the car off evaporated rapidly.

I had to give various fatuous details like my name and address to some police message-clearing centre. By the time an alert reached Camberwell the car would be in Croydon. Imagine if it were more serious; 'I, Jim Parton, no, not Jim Parsons, Parton as in the buxom singer, ha, ha, ha, of Twenty-eight Dunroamin' Villas, yes, 'n' apostrophe, am fending off a frenzied axe murderer, could you come and save me?'

Having the same surname as Dolly Parton is quite handy. For some reason, certain types of people find it hilarious to call me

Dolly. For my part, I find this tendency a useful and infallible index as to whether or not my interlocutor is a prat.

The car had only been a company car, but its theft was a serious blow to the skiing holiday.

It was Friday, and the last morning meeting before freedom. The disappointing demise of my car didn't stop me making some brilliant remarks about Hermès ties and the ex-Army officer's need for conformity. The electronics analyst with the gravy stains found me amusing, and I even raised a faint titter from the exponent of the dismal science.

There was news that Ron the redundant market maker had got another job already, and would be starting with a Japanese securities house on Monday. That made just two weeks unemployed. I thought he was off his head; I could never understand the urgency some people had to pile back into work when they had just received a fat redundancy cheque and could therefore take a nice long holiday.

Giussi asked why it was that the unpronounceable Swedish stock, which had risen another eight per cent since Mr Hoshide's sale, making a total of twenty, was going up when our analyst had said it was a sell.

'More buyers than sellers, Giussi,' came an irony laden chorus from around the table. This is stockbroker speak for 'We don't know'.

It would take Giussi about a year to work out that stock analysts' earnings forecasts are rarely right and that even when they are, it is just as rare for the shares to react in the way expected. There are just too many unpredictable variables such as Berlin Wall falls (shares rise, border guard gets crushed), Saddam invades Kuwait (shares fall, plump Arabs flee), unemployment increases for the tenth month running (shares do nothing at all), general panic occurs for no identifiable reason (shares crash, or, just as likely, soar).

Many stockbrokers are vain enough to believe that they might be capable of supplying correct recommendations. Equally, many fund managers think they can act correctly on the recommendations, or cleverly disagree with them. A dartboard is a more valuable tool than a fund manager's judgement, because at least then you save his monstrous fees.

The discreet use of insider knowledge is the only sure way of beating the dartboard. Contrary to popular opinion, this is surprisingly rare. I don't think I was ever in possession of this kind of information, in a form in which I could act on it and make myself a fortune. I once acted on a tip that a company was going to be taken over, but it turned out to be wrong.

There are occasional successes by analysts. Derek Terrington at UBS Phillips and Drew was not allowed to express his fears about Maxwell because the corporate finance department were touting for business. Instead he wrote, 'Can't Recommend A Purchase – Hold', an acronymical way of telling clients what he really thought. (A good analyst, he is no longer at P & D. The analyst who was so keen on Polly Peck still works there.)

Ads for unit trusts mention that 'the value of investments can go down as well as up'. They ought to carry the warning that seventy per cent of professionally-managed funds underperform the indices they are trying to beat. Unit trusts are bad for your wealth.

I have yet to see a study that proved that professional fund manager 'A', or his company, consistently turns in superior performances in all market conditions. Any fund manager with a couple of years at the top of his table is sensible to use the opportunity to move to a higher paid job, because it is improbable that his luck will last. The chances are that he will move, not through a cynical understanding of what little value his abilities have, but through a genuine belief that he is worth more than he is paid. And brokers, of course, encourage this vanity; if they can get a client into a bigger institution it means more commission for them.

The fund manager himself spends his whole working life being fawned upon by brokers, and ends up with the genuine belief that he is witty, companionable, and highly analytical, and the mildest wimps become quite intolerably arrogant. Any given stockbroking salesman actively dislikes nine out of ten fund managers, frequently his best client most of all.

Alick used to put it this way: 'Would you invite your clients home for dinner?' And the answer, in his case, was only two of them from a list of twenty or so. I don't think I am damaging his business prospects in revealing this; the other eighteen will all believe they are one of the two.

It is a funny relationship. Fund managers look down upon brokers because they believe themselves to be brighter. Brokers look down on fund managers for being so dumb as to be fund managers and therefore paid considerably less.

Until the Gulf War at least, Alick's biggest and best client was a no-flies-on-me East Ender at the Kuwait Investment Office, called Bernie. The K.I.O. had massive funds (slightly less post-Saddam), and for such a fund to make meaningful investments, they had to be big. At Christmas, Alick sent Bernie a book, *Blood in the Streets* by Lord Rees-Mogg. It has turned out to be rather prescient, predicting crashes, and the current slump. Bernie rang back and said, 'I don't want a fucking book, send us some wine.' Alick sent him some wine.

Because of the size of the orders, and the ferocity of Bernie, Alick would run around like a headless chicken each time he got one, in a panic that it wasn't executed properly by the dealers. I lost count of the number of times that Alick was threatened with being struck off Bernie's small list of preferred brokers. I think this salesman-client relationship worked because Bernie, the barrow boy, got a kick out of pushing Alick, the Old Etonian, around.

Fund managers get paid bonuses in relation to performance against a yardstick such as the FTSE 100 index, whereas brokers get a bonus related to the amount of commission they make, which is unrelated to any index, only the level of activity. We brokers can develop selective memories if we have the misfortune for example, to recommend a Polly Peck or a Maxwell shortly before it collapses. For us to advise such an investment carries no personal risk whatsoever, whereas for a fund manager to follow the advice could set his career back quite severely. Giving advice is risk free, taking it is fraught with danger.

I assume that all this is pretty fundamental stuff to anyone who works in the City, but maybe not. I was constantly surprised at brokers who were genuinely indignant when fund managers didn't give them business despite 'brilliant' recommendations. If they really knew which stocks were going to go up they wouldn't altruistically pass this information on. They would all be retired millionaires.

For the record, in my time, apart from getting the oil price right in the Gulf War, I have earnestly recommended Polly Peck (my employers Phillips and Drew were particularly keen on it at the time), Maxwell and other disaster areas, all at their peak. I also bought an expensive house in 1989, thinking it was near the bottom of the market, and made a decision to back the Japanese and their money in 1986. This last had served me well, but time was running out.

On hearing the sad fate of my car, Alick asked his usual 'Was it a black man, Dolly?' As somebody who occasionally smuggled in a copy of the *Guardian* in a brown paper bag to read on the loo, it irritated me to have to reply in the affirmative.

Fortunately half a dozen people in the bond department had been fired recently so the company car man was able to offer me an immediate replacement. He was very understanding about my having left the keys in the ignition. 'Would have done it myself, mate.' His pay was obviously not linked to insurance premiums for his cars.

He offered me the loan of a Vauxhall Astra GTE, one year old, lots of valves, 8,500 miles. It had seen better days, with special features like jagged holes for the various stolen radio components, scrape marks from parking misjudgements or errant supermarket trolleys, a forlorn stump for an ex wing mirror and doors that could only be opened from the outside. The ashtrays were full, so the floor had been used instead.

It was a typical company car.

6

I assembled my ski team and two cars at home in Camberwell. Dramatis Personae. Skiing holiday. (Final.)

1. Me. Brilliant skier.
2. Wife. Rotten skier.
3. Niall. Ski soulmate of old. Brilliant skier.
4. Alick. Friend and boss; in which order, unsure. Claim to be a brilliant skier as yet unaudited.
5. Chip. Young American disco soulmate of wife. Unknown quantity.
6. Verona. Beginner. Extremely glamorous if tired-looking youngest ever director of Breese, Spotch and Betts. Terrifying advertising exec.
7. Sienna. Beginner. Sister to the above. Willowy tennis pro, too British and not butch enough for Wimbledon.

By 1 a.m. we were South of Reims. Driving through the night was gruelling, but the autoroutes were almost deserted. We had a deal whereby if one car was stopped by the police for speeding, the on-the-spot fine would be divided across all passengers in both cars, which enabled us to drive at 120mph. March is not too bad a time of year for French speed cops; the real danger time is around Christmas when they need a bit of pocket money for presents for their mistresses.

I needn't have worried because Verona refused to let anyone drive her Maserati at anything other than a very unItalian eighty-five mph, which was just as well because the Astra needed an oil change every petrol stop. I suspect it had never been serviced by its Merrill Lynch salesman, or, not to be sexist, saleswoman.

Arrived at the Cowshed at six in the morning, knackered. Outside it was minus five degrees Celsius.

Step One: I spent ten minutes while everyone shivered introducing the key into the lock, which was obviously frozen. I suggested using duty-free Scotch to thaw it. Niall objected on the grounds of economy and sacrilege. The girls started to cry. As team leader, I took command, and we compromised on gin. Inside it was minus ten degrees Celsius.

Step Two: Referred to Major Parton's (Dad's) Cowshed operating instructions. We had owned this property for ten years in which time it had expanded into a monster of Byzantine complexity as a result of my father's DIY fantasies confused with his concept of military precision.

Step Three: Chip moved all the gas heaters into one bedroom. The girls all went to bed as did Chip. Niall volunteered to help me, but realising that we were dealing with Parton technology I sent him to bed too.

Step Four: Turned on the water system, which had been carefully drained to avoid the problem of frozen pipes. Opted for option E. 'Kitchen with all three bathrooms; for larger and/or richer parties.' We fitted into the latter category. 'Open stopcock A, close stopcock G (in hole in panelling between lavatory and basin in far bathroom, ensure stopcocks C, D, and E, are open, close system draining taps (behind a hole in the back of the kitchen unit behind sliding door).'

Water now flowed in most basins, although not all, implying the odd ice blockage somewhere.

Step Five: 'Section C, Annex A. Please ensure that all members of your party read this section of the instructions and follow them to the letter.' I hadn't the heart; it could wait till the morning, not least because there was a block of ice in each of the loos. I let the girls sleep.

The time was about half past six.

It was two hours later, half past eight. 'Hey man, let's kick butt.' Chip was up brewing coffee. Keen, enthusiastic, American, and only twenty-three, he wanted to go skiing. Immediately. 'Up yours.' Some British irony was not entirely lost on him.

It was another two hours later. Half past ten.

'Hey man, let's kick butt.' Chip had been out, collected wood, built a fire, and, as an incentive to get everyone up, was brewing some more coffee. He had discovered the local shop and bought a baguette and croissants. Keen, enthusiastic, American, only twenty-three, he wanted to go skiing. Immediately. I would have just said 'Go skiing then', but the resort was five kilometres away, and he would need a car.

Niall emerged, as did I. The girls remained in bed.

An hour later, half past eleven. Chip was beginning to foam quietly at the mouth. Keen, enthusiastic, American, etc. I didn't really see this as my problem, because he was my wife's guest, but nevertheless hinted to her that she ought to get up. She and the two sisters dragged themselves out of their warm pits. Before they were fully awake I thought it safe to inform them about the block of ice in each loo, and also issued a military briefing thereon.

Section C, Annex A. Lavatories.

1.   Please ensure that all members of your party read this section of the instructions and obey them to the letter.

2.   If a lavatory bowl fails to drain, the septic tank is: either a. frozen solid or b. temporarily blocked.

3.   If (a), there is nothing you can do except consider the alternatives laid out in paragraph (7) below.

4.   If (b), take action as given in paragraph (5) below.

5.   The tank is designed to cope indefinitely with the output of four people. For limited periods (two weeks) it will cope with larger parties (10) provided that the following points are rigidly observed: a. Use a minimum amount of paper. Single thickness not double. Use only proper lavatory paper, i.e. not newspaper or kitchen paper. b. Under no circumstances should it be used for disposal of any kind of rubbish whatsoever. Not even paper handkerchiefs. Not items of personal hygiene. Nothing. GET IT?

6. Provided any blockage has been reported to the head of the household immediately, and you have not got a blockage on top of a blockage, you should be able to free it by using copious amounts of cold water and a plunger. In a 'bad case' try several times. On no account flush during this procedure if you are keen to avoid an environmental disaster.

7. If this fails, you are left with the following choices: a. Use the emergency Racasan bucket. b. The river. c. Hang on until the bottom of the téléphérique. d. Go home.

8. See also Annex A to Section A.

Annex A to Section A. The Downstairs Bathroom.

1. This bathroom is below septic tank level and so has an electric pump and shredder to raise solids to the right level at the appropriate consistency.

2. The shredder will cope with all normal lavatory solids but not with plastic or rubber. You must tell your guests about this and be utterly explicit. Experience indicates that euphemisms pass over most people's heads. The shredder is a very expensive piece of equipment. (That's enough plumbing – Ed.)

Having drawn this euphemistically to the attention of the party we were about ready to go skiing, except for a need to equip Verona and Sienna. I took them to Monsieur Noz, where I explained that they were debutantes. Noz was deeply suspicious of the new fad of shorter skis. Small details like the fact that they are easier to turn are nothing against *la stabilité*. Verona and Sienna were issued with monsters.

Beginners at skiing are not merely beginners at skiing; they have to learn how to walk with ski boots on, how to carry planks and sticks at the same time, and tricks like remembering that they stick out at the back when you put them on your shoulder, so that if you rotate through 180 degrees the bit sticking out invariably decapitates a passing Frenchman. This is how they met Pascal, a local ski instructor, with roguish Alain Prost good looks and short stature, who volunteered, having looked them up and down, to teach them.

The other thing about beginners is that they take ages putting themselves together, adjusting boot clips or bindings. To kill time, Chip had bought lip salve, mirror sun glasses, a new pair of gloves, and a coloured scarf to tie round his knee. He had also had the bottoms of his skis hot waxed and the edges sharpened, and having ascertained the correct local frequency for his avalanche bleeper was saying things like 'Let's kick butt', with the time lag between each utterance diminishing, like the minor shocks before a major earthquake.

It being well past one o'clock by now, Rika suggested that it was time for lunch. A nice restaurant with a sixty-seven franc menu including half bottle of wine beckoned. I was in a dilemma because I had signed a charter to do whatever my wife wanted, but on the other hand her friend, if he didn't get skiing soon, would start having some kind of a seizure. Although I was now thirty-one, I still remember the frustrations of being twenty-three. I ordered us up the mountain.

On the first day of a skiing holiday a series of 'species recognition' dances takes place, which are much worse than the strains one's unfit body is subjected to. The women had already eyed each other's anoraks and admired various features in the way only women can do when they have a point to make. 'C & A are making some lovely things these days,' said Rika. Pretty hard-hitting stuff, showing a sophisticated grasp, for a foreigner, of how the British middle-classes don't want to be suspected of overdressing. Verona's riposte of 'Gorgeous design, lovely feel, but you must have had to take out a mortgage on it,' was water off a duck's back. It is a peculiar British virtue to be seen not to be trying. Large sums of money spent on clothes were not something my wife had difficulty coming to terms with. That was left to me and my bank manager, a sympathetic fellow who recognised that my earnings made me capable of supporting quite a lot of debt.

We men eyed each other's skis. No contest there. Niall's were two metres fifteen centimetres long, he had bought them from a member of the British ski team who had had some spare from his sponsor. Chip's were not especially long, but they were made of Kevlar by the box torsion zeta method, and matched the scarf round his knee. He pressed the bottoms lovingly to his cheek as we went up the cable car. Mine were a good second-hand pair bought off some flash bastard who wanted to graduate onto this year's colours.

Chip flew neatly down the mountain with a cry of 'Hey man, let's kick butt'. An alarmingly good skier, Niall eschewed style; he could afford to because he had the longest and therefore most manly pair of skis, too massive for threading through the bumps, he bounced over them touching only where gravity dictated. He had the assurance of someone who didn't need to show off. As for myself, kind people call it 'spectacular' – legs and arms everywhere. I don't see how you can be six foot four, possess size thirteen feet, and be tidy. Purists have trouble coming to terms with this style, but it works.

It is extremely galling to report, however, that Chip was better than me. Rika viewed the battle from the side of the piste having taken the blue run down, satisfied that her protégé was humiliating her husband.

We only managed a couple of hours before it was time to go in.

Verona and Sienna were looking flushed with success. Pascal had told them that they had natural talent, apparently referring to their skiing.

Back at the Cowshed, things were not quite what they might have been. Water cascaded down the stairs and through the floors. Carpets, upholstered furniture, bags of sugar, lentils, all saturated, rivers of Weetabix on the floor along with soggy baguettes floating like escaped turds at the Thames Barrier.

I discovered that I had overlooked Annex P (3) of the Cowshed operating instructions and failed to close down system draining tap G. Also, a block of ice in the upstairs lavatory cistern had melted sufficiently to allow the ballcock to descend and supply it with water. This would have been fine if the aforementioned block of ice had not cracked said cistern thereby making the supply everlasting. The only double bed was soaked, a severe blow to a working man normally too exhausted to do anything but sleep in one, and still clinging to the vain hope of luring Rika into it. It would take about a month to dry.

There is a myth that Orientals are inscrutable. Rika speaks very good English, particularly when roused, and handles certain idioms very skilfully. I think she caught the mood of the occasion perfectly when she described me as a 'Fucking idiot'.

None of the women were of the tough outward-bound variety, so I realised it was in my interests to suggest that they spent the night in the local auberge while we men sorted things out. Chip volunteered to help them with their bags and skis.

The temperature inside had crept up to about three degrees Celsius, enough to melt the plug of ice leading to system draining tap G, but not exactly what was needed after a vigorous day's exercise in the cold. Still, Niall is a genuine Scotsman from a cold bothy in the Highlands and as team leader I had no choice.

We had supper at the auberge; Chip and the girls looked refreshed after long baths. Then it was early to bed having scotched a move by Chip to 'kick butt' in a disco.

7

Outside it was ten degrees, bad news for the snow, inside still not quite as warm, but getting there. It is a charming feature of traditional Savoyard properties with four-foot-thick stone walls that they retain the temperature of the coldest snap that winter.

I had a depressing day on the slopes. My body wouldn't do what it was told, whereas Chip's body appeared to do everything demanded of it. Niall was still a great skier. He had become a lot smoother since St Andrews and said that he hadn't fallen for three years, a considerable improvement, because if anything had divided us it was the fact that he fell a lot and I didn't. Clearly for the last three years he hadn't been trying hard enough. I was reduced to lying to Chip that I used to be better than Niall at university. 'Yes, I can see that you were a very good skier once, James, but you're looking a bit stiff. Try leaning forward a bit more.' I hate people who call me James only marginally less than people who call me Dolly.

We met Verona and Sienna in a café drinking vin chaud and genepi with Pascal, who reaffirmed that they were 'very good', still apparently referring to their skiing. They had an air of contentment.

Physically-speaking the end of the second day is always the worst. Taking ski boots off is a torture that the manufacturers have yet to find a way around, so most of us opted to get into the two cars with them on. Verona's Maserati, being convertible, was ideal for piling skis into. Verona demonstrated why her rise at Breese, Spotch and Betts had been so meteoric: she ordered us and the skis out. She was worried about the leather seats. I pointed out that it was a company car. What would it matter if a bit of snow melted onto them and they got a trifle scuffed, especially as she never sat in the back anyway. She couldn't be persuaded to see it this way.

I did manage to persuade the women and Chip that the Cowshed was now safe for occupation, which give or take the odd pool of water, it was. Even Chip had his uses. He was very good at hewing wood and building fires and soon had one big enough to roast an elk.

It was the last day for honing skills before the arrival of Alick. I was convinced that I was as good as Chip, but my body was holding me back. I'd lost my nerve, I thought twice about doing things, quite a shock to me, who had previously been fearless. At the tender age of thirty-one, no older than Linford Christie, or Gary Lineker, considerably younger than Jimmy Connors or Franz Klammer when he retired, I was held back by an inability to commit myself, and by knees without the correct shock-absorbing qualities. Not being able to hold my own against a twenty-three-year-old was an unexpected blow. When I got back I promised myself a new regime; squash twice a week, running, sit-ups and press-ups before bed.

I offered to teach Rika, who I had more or less ignored so far in the battle to beat Chip. She couldn't fail to be delighted. 'Chip's much more stylish than you and Niall,' she said, rejecting my offer. I was beginning to hate Chip.

The snow was getting distinctly patchy: roots, rocks, myrtille bushes all appearing, so the final ski down was really for the foolhardy only, which included all of us men who were still trying to prove things to each other. Rika went down on the chairlift. Only those who had skied a lot in Scotland would regard the conditions as good. 'Hey man, this is different,' said Chip, before regaling us with stories of heli-skiing in the Bugaboos. I had provided him with a pleasant piece of rural France to stay in, sorry I couldn't provide the helicopter.

Verona and Sienna had had another successful day and had invited Pascal to dinner the next night.

In the evening we prepared a cauldron of boeuf bourguignon. The only thing that anyone could remember about the recipe was that it required a lot of red wine.

Outside, rain was gently falling which was likely to be disastrous for the snow unless the temperature dropped suddenly.

8.17 p.m. I went to meet Alick's train from Lyon, but he wasn't on it.

9.17 p.m. Neither was he on the one an hour later.

10.47 p.m. Nor, come to that, on the final one. I concluded that

Merrill Lynch must have got busy, or that Bernie the barrow boy had given him a large order that the dealers had messed up, and he had been unavoidably detained, or that perhaps his wife had sprogged.

Just as I turned in for bed there was a loud knocking on the door. Ah, Alick, we thought. It turned out to be a drunken Pascal who had inexplicably lost his way to the village. We sent him on his way. '*Demain*, Pascal.' I politely but firmly told him that our womenfolk had gone to bed, although I said that Chip was available for the disco.

Five minutes later, Pascal was again at the door, muttering something about his *voiture*. It turned out that he had driven it off the road above the house and been very lucky to avoid a cold, wet and premature death in the River Isère. I drove him to the village where his mate was woken to retrieve it with his tractor, before the arrival of the flics, not that I had ever seen a flic in this part of the valley.

4 a.m.-ish, I think. Further loud knocking on the door, this time angry and insistent. *Va t'en, sale grenouille*, I thought.

In fact it was Alick. The poor fellow had misread my instructions and got off at Bourg St Maurice instead of the station before. He said my directions were very ambiguous. When he started his quest to find us there had been a few taxis about, but towards midnight he ran out of transport, so laden with skis and bags he spent a happy few hours waking up Frenchmen asking '*Où est la maison de Monsieur Parton*,' in his Army officer French, before eventually falling in with a jolly chap with a bruised face muttering something about his *voiture* and resembling Alain Prost. A large quantity of eau de vie from an unmarked bottle later, and it emerged that we were well known in this area. '*Ah, oui, les Parton, là-bas*,' at which the jolly man collapsed. Alick walked in the direction of the prostrate figure's arm, and eventually found us. He said he had already walked past three times earlier in the evening because it looked too agricultural.

8 a.m. Chip was noisily making coffee and building a fire, muttering 'Let's kick butt'. He was only marginally less irritating than Gen of a morning. 'Powder snow,' he said, and sure enough the apple trees outside had acquired a gentle dusting of the fluffy stuff, meaning that 800 metres higher in the resort, conditions would be great. Early though it was, I felt galvanised. I felt a bit sorry for Alick, who, on five hours sleep and a hangover must have been knackered, but he would understand.

Alick brought me up to date on developments at work. Amongst other things, he was pleased to say that they had been able to hire that Nordic person, the one they had described as 'a bit of a bandit'. Being on holiday, I wasn't terribly interested, but it did pass through my mind that there would have to be some upheaval on the seating front. If I played my cards right, I would end up sitting next to Giussi.

Seven people, two cars. Not an unmanageable equation in normal circumstances, but Verona was adamant that be-ski booted men would not be allowed in her car. Three women got into the Maserati, (rechristened Masturbati by its growing number of detractors), four men into the Astra. With the ban on skis in the Maserati, the four men were made to share their space with seven pairs of skis, which stuck out of the sunroof.

The Maserati set off first, as finding a configuration for putting the skis through the sunroof which didn't interfere with the gearstick and handbrake delayed the departure of our car. We encountered it halfway up the mountain, stuck in the new snow. Masturbatis don't go up icy mountains very easily. Verona had no chains. Neither did we, but being four heavy men and seven pairs of skis and having front wheel drive, we gripped very nicely. I impressed upon Verona the importance of correct weight distribution, dodged the ensuing slap, and explained that I was referring to the car. I succeeded in having two men and seven pairs of skis transferred into the back. We made it to the slopes, hee, hee.

Pascal was still pissed, concussed, or both and therefore hors de combat, which meant that we were stuck with the two beginners who we agreed to meet for lunch at the top of the mountain. Chip was under strict instructions not to ski better than Alick. Overnight there had been two feet of powder, and at the top we emerged through the clouds into the sun to look down onto valleys filled with cotton wool. Chip weaved perfectly regular, rhythmic, snake-like tracks down the mountain. He was kicking butt. Niall did the same, except that his tracks had gaps because he spent so much time in the air. The two feet of powder was on a base of rock-hard ice, and I couldn't take the strain, it was my thirty-one-year-old stockbroker's knees playing up again.

Alick attempted to weave similar tracks to Chip's. He was in first day species recognition mode. He took a purler and got up looking like an Old English sheepdog. He roared with laughter, but a vein throbbing in his forehead told of a deeper-seated angst. I cast Chip a sharp admonitory glance but he was already 500 yards down the slope kicking butt.

Arriving at the top again, I had just about recuperated enough for the next run down. Having established that Chip was fitter and generally better than myself, I thought I might as well allow Alick to discover the same thing before showing him that he was not first in the pecking order as he was apparently used to, not even second, but a devastating fourth.

The usually ebullient Alick was oddly quiet at lunchtime. He started going on about being a qualified Army ski instructor and volunteered to give the girls a lesson. There was as yet no sign of the latter; 'The best laid plans of mice and men gang aft a-gley' as Niall might have put it were it not gobbledegook, and he not from Edinburgh Morningside.

Having colonised a nice patch in the sun with a splendid view, fought through the queue, purchased saucisses, frites and as they say in Morningside, an elegant sufficiency of wine, we waited. And waited. Scrounged some abandoned wine from the next table then waited some more. No Verona and Sienna.

Chip began to get restless. He wanted to go skiing again. Me too. I felt fortified. Rika was content to lie in the sun; she is very attractive and it wouldn't be too long before some unctuous Frog tried to pick her up.

Back on the slopes, Niall and I pulverised Chip, and Alick was left standing. I had discovered the missing *je ne sais quoi*: wine. All the old skills came back, the ability to turn a seemingly lost situation into a spectacular recovery, to spray passing Germans with snow. The box torsion zeta method was no match for me.

The two sisters had arrived by the time we regained the top. There was no sign of Rika, who was probably queuing for the ladies. This always takes a good half hour in ski resorts because there is only ever one cupboard-sized loo. Rika says that the gymnastics required to undo the salopettes and get into a decent squatting position without getting them wet in the melted snow on the cubicle floor are spectacular.

The sisters were distinctly unimpressed by our non-presence. They had just spent two and a half hours trying to find the restaurant. I had given them unambiguous instructions to take the chairlift up on the left, and they had taken me at my word, except that they had been coming up when they followed the instructions and I had been pointing down when I gave them.

Alick was not in butt-kicking mode; I think he fancied stroking it. He was left teaching the women whilst Niall, Chip and I had a fabulous 'boys only' afternoon.

Later on, following Chip and Niall down a steep and narrow slope, I lost control. I can remember going too fast, and then waking up in the snow with no idea where I was, or what had happened, and being on my own. All I knew was that I had to find Chip and Niall, and that I should ski down, which I was able to do.

'Chip, where are you?' doesn't have quite the resonance of 'Heathcliffe'. The only clue as to what had happened to me was a bruise on my nose and a dent in my side.

I found Chip. 'Chip, where am I?' By this stage, events from the morning were coming back to me; I could remember Alick's throbbing vein, but I couldn't remember which resort I was in.

Chip took me to a clinic to have my head X-rayed, and my memory gradually came back. The doctor said I needed observing constantly and should be woken up at regular intervals in the night to check that I was still alive. We paid him an outrageous sum of money for this advice then went down to the Cowshed in a taxi, Niall being despatched to the other side of the resort to tell the others what had happened, not to wait for me, and to drive the cars down. Basically I was all right, the worst thing about it was being looked after so nicely and considerately by Chip, and the vindication of Alick's decision to give the girls a ski lesson.

Back at the Cowshed everybody was quite knackered. Not even Chip was campaigning for a trip to the disco. People either had their noses in thick novels, or were dribbling into them having fallen asleep. On doctor's orders I wasn't allowed to go to sleep in case I didn't wake up again.

Verona had volunteered to do the cooking. I think she had only ever opened a Marks & Spencer's packet and popped it in the microwave in her life before, and she clearly regarded the whole process as a bit of a joke, and a novelty. Eating is one of the things I do best, and commensurate with that talent is one for cooking. I made sure there was loads of mince in the spag-bog she was preparing, and enjoyed her expression when I told her it was horse.

Pascal arrived. We had forgotten about him, after all he had been too ill to make it to work. However, after a day in bed he was fully recovered. I too, had fully recovered my faculties by this stage, but had a splitting headache, and an incomplete set of stigmata, namely a hole in my side, not from a Roman legionary's spear, but probably a ski binding. Pascal produced an unmarked bottle of eau de vie as a gift and aperitif. '*Cadeau de mon grand-père,*' he said, before pouring himself a large slug and passing it around like a cigarette with illicit substances in it. The local moonshine.

It turned out that Pascal had lived in this very house when he was small, or rather smaller, because, Alain Prost-like, he was still small. It had belonged to his extended family until the day we had fetched up and bought it from his grandfather for £4,000, twelve years ago. He had lived here with grandparents, parents, four brothers and two sisters. He was very complimentary about my father's DIY efforts. In his day the cows were kept directly beneath, in the place where we now kept the skis and the wine. Before the family became rich in the ski boom, the cows had been an integral part of the central heating system. Now they had moved into a well-insulated, modern building made of concrete, faced with wood for authenticity.

Interesting though all this social history was, I got the impression that Verona was losing interest rapidly. I don't think she had had too much to do with genuine peasants in her life, and was beginning to regret inviting him to supper. She must have been taken in by his ski clothes. I guess Johnny Europeasant knows how to dress up: it is difficult to imagine Eddie Grundy in Armani.

I helped her unstick the spaghetti, and suggested a few herbs to add to the bolognese sauce. '*À table*, dinner is served.'

Noses emerged from novels, bodies from beds. Pascal was in tremendous form, having spent the whole day lying in bed. Bottles of plonk were distributed around the table. '*Produit de plusieurs pays de la communauté européenne.*' Not even the local plonk.

After a day in the cold doing unaccustomed exercise everybody was ravenous, so it didn't matter that Verona had burnt the bolognese. It was head down, nose in trough, revolve jaws, emerge for a swig of red wine, nose down again. Pascal was irrepressibly cheery, and had clearly been hair-of-the-dogging since well before he arrived. '*Putain*' (local argot for 'Gosh' and not a reflection of the women assembled in front of him), '*Délicieux*'. He complimented Verona on her kitchen. '*Vous faites bien la cuisine.*' Bovine grunts of approval from around the table. Verona looked at Pascal with a look of renewed appreciation of his Alain Prost-like good looks.

He turned to me. '*Elle parle français*' indicating my wife with his nose.

'*Non.*' I replied.

'*Ca baise bien, n'est ce pas, les Japonaises,*' he opined, somewhat impertinently, given that we were dealing with my spouse.

'Yes, they kiss very well,' I replied in English.

Rika smiled benignly. She had had three glasses of red wine, and was not entirely with it. Everything one hears about the Japanese not being able to take their alcohol is true, except that in Rika's case she doesn't get wild and silly, she gets quiet and silly then falls asleep. I gave her about fifteen minutes.

Sure enough she was soon collapsed into her spaghetti at the end of the table. A combination of altitude, alcohol, skiing and this irrepressible Frenchman. I gave her a fireman's lift up the stairs. Pascal winked knowingly, unaware that I might be suffering from brain damage and could die at any time, and of the design of the bunk beds and the sodden state of the one double bed. My wife was completely safe from molestation.

The stairs were apparently original and used to lead to the hay loft where Pascal *avait souvent fait dans le hay loft ce qu'on fait dans le hay loft* (or so he said).

By the time I got downstairs again Pascal was virtually alone, having bored everyone to bed, with the exception of Chip who appeared from the cattle byre below clutching his skis, with the intention of having an animated discussion about wax and edges, and whether kevlar was as good as teflex. Pascal decided it was time to leave, the women were all in bed, and talking skiing would remind him too much of work.

My night's sleep was broken once every two hours by Chip, worried that I might die, to ask how many fingers he was holding up. My joke of looking puzzled then saying 'four' when he held up two backfired on me because he then started waking me up once an hour.

* * *

8 a.m. Chip was up making coffee, with the rest of the party determined to lie in. He told me I wasn't allowed coffee, which was a blessing, because I could lie in. I was beginning to realise that it was in everyone's interest for him to be encouraged to go out to the disco, and twitch away until dawn.

8.15 a.m. Everybody else was up, woken by a combination of file rasping along edges, and the smell of molten ski wax.

I had a day off, before rejoining the circus. Alick drove off to Courchevel to look at a new development of flats on which to spend his bonus. Lots of guff about needing to be right on the slopes so that his children could pitch in and out. This may have been so, but the real reason was that in Courchevel they have a better class of vowel. Our two destinations tend to be Les Arcs, with lots of Essex types on packages, and La Plagne, massively overpopulated with Germans.

A few days later a telegram came for Rika summoning her to Venice (or was it Cannes?) for some must-do-now filming. We don't have a telephone in the Cowshed, but somehow she had been tracked down, or more likely, it was a set-up to escape.

Our skiing was developing a pattern. I was pretty much rehabilitated, and after ten days or so was skiing well. On the one-franc-in-the-slot automatic slalom course at La Plagne I reigned supreme. Chip might be able to beat me down something requiring nerve, but on something where skill was the criterion, I could teach the young man a thing or two. Ha!

His holiday too was at an end, and we said goodbye to him. In the visitors' book he wrote 'Hey, man, sure as hell liked your cowshed!! It's kinna neat?!? James, kick butt, but mind your head!!!' Prat.

My father has a pathological dislike of people who write comments in his visitors' book, and I guess I can see his point. I have a dread of other people's visitors' books. I have a particular aversion to exclamation marks. When you are confronted with that blank column at the end, the pressure to write something witty and apposite invariably leads to it coming out merely idiotic. At the Cowshed, under Section D (5) of the operating instructions, it says 'Under no account will you allow your guests to write comments in the visitors' book. This is reserved for items of historical interest only.' Entries are restricted to 'Upstairs back room sex-proof bunk beds completed, 3/6/81.' When my father visits he solemnly goes through the book Tipp-Exing out all other comments.

The snow was fast melting, and some runs were only for the foolhardy like ourselves. Niall had a distinct advantage here, being used to Aviemore, where you bounce from heather to sheet of ice taking in the occasional patch of snow. It was the end of the day, and we were near the bottom of the resort. 'Och, I remember this bit,' he said, pulling up ahead of a patch of snow, rock, and semi-submerged logs, with the piste forty yards beyond across the slush.

He couldn't possibly have remembered 'this bit'. It was ten years ago, and ten years ago there was always lots of snow, falling over didn't hurt. He turned over the first rock, landing briefly on the patch of heavy slush beyond, hurdled a felled pine tree, strung together three deft turns over obstacles out of my view and landed on the piste.

If he could do it, so could I. And so I did. Looking back at what I had just done and seeing some of the lurking dangers I had unknowingly avoided I realised what a nut he was: in a different class from Chip.

For Alick the rhythm was never quite established. He got over the rock but misjudged the hurdle, and the three deft turns were never there. We looked up to see him in an intimate embrace with a fir tree, shouting 'My knee'. The lifts were closing so we went down.

Next day Alick had a rest day, and borrowed the car to go and have another look at apartments in Courchevel. The swelling on his knee looked ominous. I knew the outcome of this, having done it myself – I still wear a massive knee brace – his holiday was finished. He decided to go home to be with his pregnant wife. In the visitors' book he wrote, 'Dolly, shame you can't broke stocks as well as you broke your head!!' Quite witty for Alick.

I was sad to see him go. We were all just getting into it, and I regretted not having had the opportunity to have a frank man-to-man chat with him on the chairlift about what sort of pressure he was under to have me let go. The 'long term' for Merrill Lynch was notoriously fluid in meaning.

From here on in, the holiday started to wind quietly down. The girls disappeared to Paris in the Maserati. Verona had a Trans Manche Link with a young man there, and needed a service. Her contribution to the sales of Tipp-Ex was 'Jim knocked himself out; of historical interest!?!'

Niall and I were left for a final blast down the mountainside, unfettered by the need to show off or be shown off to. I was thoroughly wound down from the City pressure cooker, and in no mood to crank myself up again for it. I hadn't thought of the markets once, hadn't bought a newspaper, was only dimly aware of what the date was.

In the visitors' book, Niall wrote 'Jim you're a headcase on skis!'

We had a lovely drive back through France on side roads, loading the car with all the kinds of things that cost half what they would in England. Coffee, Belgian chocolate, olive oil, gourmet cans (cheaper than the Chinese takeaway), smoked ham, decent cheese, and of course, an elegant sufficiency of red wine (right thinking plonk drinkers only drink red).

As we approached Calais it clouded over, then the wind started to buffet the car, then it actually started raining. By the time we were on the ferry it was a full-scale tempest. The rain continued to London. Somehow this seemed to happen every time I made this journey, and I told myself that I must give up living in London, and working in the City. I would have a suntan for two weeks after which no one would even be able to tell that I had been on holiday, and neither would I feel as if I had.

Niall went back to Scotland. We promised each other we would do the British ski championship next year; it was a long-standing ambition to do a real downhill and the biological clock was ticking against us.

I spent the next day recovering. At no stage of a skiing holiday does your body fully recover from all its bruises and strains. Thank God for God. It was Easter Monday, and there was no need to go to work.

8

I knew I was back from my holiday when I made the traditional discovery of the lack of an ironed shirt.

I felt unenthusiastic about work so I passed the day calling no clients whatsoever, and caught up on the two weeks of economic and company news I had missed. In my absence, my desk had been relocated out of the compact group of four salesmen. I was now next to the settlements girl, Mimi, so that, it was explained, Giussi could sit next to the other three, to learn the ropes a bit more easily. The settlements girl would shortly be found a place nearby on her own, to accommodate the Nordic bandit. This seemed a bit unfair on the diligent, hyper-efficient girl, who, I reflected, was a far more crucial member of the team than me, because settling large deals inefficiently is the quickest way to lose good clients. Mimi was particularly good at pre-disarming Bernie, with her pukka Benenden vowels, before he was able to allege that Alick had ripped him off with a price.

Alick himself was still limping, but seemed in good humour.

* * *

On the second day I grasped a few nettles like calling clients and telling them I was available for business. Overnight the Dow Jones index had closed up sixty-four points, a sizeable move, at 2945. I looked at my diary and discovered that on the last day before going on holiday it had been down three points at 2946, which shows how futile all the intervening activity had been.

I was to meet Alick's boss in the afternoon to discuss a game plan for dealing with the Japanese in their quiet patch. My view was that Tokyo was the best option, despite the long hours and the proximity to my mother-in-law.

'Did ya have a good vacation James?' he asked between draws on his Romeo y Julieta. A few pleasantries were exchanged, and mention made of the sad end to Alick's holiday.

'How's business going, James?'

Well, having just got back, it had to be said, not at all. But in any case, right from the first interview eight months ago I had been dead honest about this. It would not be possible to make money from the Japanese in London on European equities for quite a while. The money was in Tokyo. But we were professionals, we knew this, and Merrill Lynch were building for the long term.

'Not very well,' I answered and explained about the deleterious effect of the Gulf War on biz, and the fact that it was not immediately obvious why my Japanese clients should trade European shares through an American broker.

'How do you think it is going to develop over the next six months, James?'

'Not very well,' and I explained how the Japanese financial system was in deep shit as a result of twenty years of borrowing money and speculating with it; fine while markets and property were going up but now that they were weak it meant that there was none spare for putting overseas, although they still did a reasonable trade with their existing portfolios out of Tokyo.

Alick's boss explained that he had costed sending me to Tokyo and it was too expensive, and candidly admitted that Merrill Lynch were having enough trouble selling US shares out there, let alone European ones.

He looked out of the window. 'In these circumstances, James, we feel your activity needs refocusing.'

I could not help but agree. For the time being, what I did would seem to need a bit of focus. We must tackle this problem.

He said that for a US firm it made more sense to spend money improving their pathetic attempts to sell European equities to the Americans before bothering with the Japanese. 'We have decided you need redirecting, James.'

The logic of this too was inescapable. Direction was just what I needed, and New York sounded fine. The wife would be delighted.

'Your area of expertise, for the moment, is redundant James,' he said.

Quick on the uptake these Americans, it was just what I had been explaining to him.

Because I still didn't seem to grasp what he was telling me, he was forced to stop looking out of the window, and, glancing briefly at me to check that I really did comprehend, added, 'You are redundant, here is your termination letter.'

The perception that I was about to have an unscripted encounter with a P45 dawned on me.

'What are my termination terms?' I asked.

'There is a letter waiting for you down in the personnel department. We don't have to pay you anything as you have only been here eight months, but we want to look after you.'

A letter already prepared! So why all that discussion about prospects? It must be so much easier in New York where they just say, 'You're fired'.

Back at my desk, my colleagues already knew. Alick must have been in on the decision and told them. He said that I could come in any time over the next few days and pick up my stuff and have free use of the phones to ring up headhunters and broking contacts in Tokyo.

It was all very gentlemanly. Gone were the days when you and fifty others first heard of your redundancy by reading the business pages of the *Telegraph* over somebody's shoulder on the Northern Line, which would be followed by arriving at work to find your personal belongings handed to you in a black bin liner by the security guard at the door. This method caught too many headlines, which brokers now eschewed because it undermined confidence both of the survivors and the clients. Just as many people were being sacked, but they were being dribbled out slowly. I had just been dribbled.

9

Rika had still not come back from Venice (or was it Cannes?), so I had time to psych myself up to tell her that I was redundant. I picked up Gen from Rory's and got him ready for bed. The urgency to get him down quickly so that I could have a bit of the evening to myself had somehow gone.

I slept soundly and decided not to go into Merrill Lynch the next day. I needed time to myself to think things over. While I was at home I had no fewer than three telephone calls from headhunters wanting to see me. It seemed that there was demand out there for somebody like myself. I spoke fluent (for C.V. purposes) Japanese and French, had five years' experience. I'd had a reasonable pay-off and had time on my hands. I would play the field and make sure I got a good job for the long term.

That night I was already drowsing in bed when a taxi from Heathrow decanted my wife.

I told Rika that I was redundant. She said that she was tired, didn't feel like it, added that she had a headache, and was asleep almost as her head hit the pillow.

I tossed and turned through the night rehearsing brilliant business plans which would make Merrill Lynch come to their senses and realise that they were discarding a source of massive future profits.

I was further kept awake by the realisation that this was not true. I achieved oblivion towards the small hours.

I lay in until Gen came to bounce on my head at around 8.30. I had no excuse not to give the urchin his breakfast. Rika remained fast asleep.

It suddenly came to me that 8.30 was cutting it a bit fine. School started at nine. I force-fed him two pieces of Weetabix, Strasbourg goose-style, put a tracksuit and sweater over his pyjamas, did similar for self and got him there only ten minutes late.

I bumped into Mr Gibbon from next door on his way to get his old age pension. Trotsky, a strange dog who I think may have been a Whippet-Doberman cross, sniffed suspiciously at my trouser legs and growled.

'You still on holiday, then?' he asked.

'In a manner of speaking, yes,' I replied, enigmatically.

On my return Rika was rolling balls of rice round pickled plums, with dried seaweed. Normally she ate a good Western breakfast of toast and coffee, but at times of severe stress or fatigue reverted. I was on my guard.

'Why aren't you at work? You having it off today?' she asked. Her English is excellent, but correct usage of certain adverbs still escapes her.

'In a manner of speaking.'

'Haven't you had enough holiday already?'

'You can never have too much holiday.' A controversial statement in certain Nipponese quarters. 'I told you I have been made redundant.'

'Oh,' she said, and looked pensive. 'Does that mean more pay?'

'In a manner of speaking,' (pet phrase of the morning), 'yes, but only this month.'

'Congratulations,' she said. 'Did you make a lot of commission?' A misunderstanding had evidently occurred, which for reasons of personal safety it might have been worth prolonging, but it was prudent to pre-empt palpitations developing in her House of Fraser card. I could imagine her hallucinating Hermès scarves.

'Redundant means I have lost my job, I am no longer employed', I said nervously. In Japan, the land of lifetime employment with one firm, redundancy is so rare and the shame so acute that when it does happen men continue to leave the house early in the morning so that the neighbours don't gossip, so I was expecting, metaphorically speaking, to be splattered against the wall.

'Typical,' she said and went on with her seaweed. And that was where the discussion remained.

I drove in to Merrill Lynch to pick up my things, ring round my clients to explain what had become of me and go for a farewell drink with my ex-colleagues. I decided to keep quiet about the car. I know of plenty of people who have driven company cars around for months (in one or two cases even years) after they have been made redundant, waiting for them to be called in.

Others, seething with anger, have driven their Porsches up the steps of their company, lodged it in the front door, then, having set the burglar alarm ringing, thrown the keys ostentatiously down the nearest drain. This struck me as a way of achieving only temporary catharsis. Much better to drive the Porsche and knacker it, although since it ultimately belongs to a leasing company, knackering it is not exactly revenge.

Giussi had occupied my desk. I couldn't help thinking that this was indecently hasty, it was a bit like a widow announcing her engagement to another man before the body of her first husband has been buried, and I was not a bit resentful of her asking me to explain my research filing system to her. She seemed surprised to see the three pairs of suit trousers come out of the cabinet from between 'Chemicals' and 'Consumer Goods'.

Giussi's old place had been vacated. Who for? The Nordic bandit. I hoped that my place would bring Giussi more luck than it brought me.

I plundered half a dozen biros, a stapler, a couple of calculators, a ream of A4, and loads of sticky yellow paper for Gen and got one of the secretaries to run up a C.V. for me on the word processor.

After 'work', I went for a farewell drink with Alick. Alick was very honest in admitting that he had had a hand in the redundancy, and he'd been in a very awkward position vis-à-vis the skiing. At that stage the decision had not yet been confirmed, he explained, and if the worst had come to the worst, he knew I would understand that work and play were separate, so he had come anyway. He'd tried to fend off the trigger-happy Americans, but when it had been put to him how keeping me in the team would affect everyone's bonus, he had been forced to back down.

Alick, Henry and Charlie came from Swiss Bank on a deal whereby they got to keep roughly fifteen per cent of the commission and market maker's credit they had made, which last year had been six million dollars, or three million pounds, fifteen per cent of which came to £150,000 each. Because of the Gulf War, this year had not been going as well, so four million-ish dollars minus the half a million dollars or so that my salary and overhead cost equalled three and a half million, fifteen per cent of which would come to around £90,000 each. I wasn't sure whether the strengthening of the dollar over the period was good or bad for the bonus, but assuming it was bad they were in line for a derisory £50,000 pay out on top of their basic salaries of about £70,000. Penury; it was not surprising that they didn't feel able to keep me on.

'Dolly,' said Alick, 'with your qualifications, people will be queuing up to employ you. Fluent Japanese and French, five years' experience.'

Yup, I agreed with that.

'March will just seem like a month with an extra big pay packet.'

I suppose so.

'You'll want to get a job pretty quickly. We found when we left Swiss Bank that two months out of the market was too long. It gets a bit boring at home all the time, missing the action.'

Completely wrong.

I never could understand this attitude. When I was recruited by Merrill Lynch I accepted a waiving of the three-month notice period I had had with Phillips and Drew, in order to start as soon as possible. I wouldn't make that mistake again.

'Why don't you get a job in fund management, Jim, or go back to Phillips and Drew?' suggested Alick, who still thought P & D had been sad to lose me. Very rude. He was inadvertently revealing his true feelings about my professional abilities. I guess I couldn't complain. I'd had five years on the City gravy train and finally been found out, but I was pretty certain I could work my magic on some new firm. Being fired by Merrill Lynch is like a badge of battle in the City. No one could hold it against me.

'Well Dolly, best of luck, although I am sure you don't need it. When I've got my apartment at Courchevel, you can drive across and we can ski together again.'

Not sure about that. 'Yes, that's a good idea, Alick.'

The City is a small and incestuous place and who knew when I would need him again; not least I wanted glowing references when his mates rang him up to ask 'You know that bloke you fired the other day, should we employ him?'

We shook hands, and he limped away.

10

I hadn't realised how difficult it was to process a small child for school and take less than an hour over it. Most people's four-year-olds wake up at six then tear around yelling. Ours seemed to have inherited the sleep gene, so task number one was to wake him up. If done too brutally Gen was too grumpy for breakfast, but if he didn't eat his breakfast he was too grumpy to go to school.

The teacher told me that one of the central tenets of the school's 'Charter for a Bright Young Future', which I apparently signed last term, was punctuality. I told her I would work on it.

'Long holidays you City types have, then' said Mr Gibbon as I passed him on the way back from school. A frail-looking man, he was still strong enough to restrain Trotsky from lunging at me too menacingly.

I dropped in on Nigel, similarly redundant stockbroker, erstwhile competitor and friend, and swapped notes. He thought that my redundancy terms of two months' pay gross after only eight months in the company were very reasonable. Most other people said the same thing. As the personnel man at Merrill Lynch had said, they didn't have to give me anything at all, and as Alick had remarked, a two-month pay off would feel like an extra bonus because I would soon be in work again.

The only thing that didn't quite ring true was Merrill Lynch's uncharacteristic attack of decency in giving me any money at all.

Nigel was waiting to start a new job and they were going to pay him twenty per cent more than he had been earning when he was sacked. No doubt something similar would happen to me; broking firms were still shelling out crazy money for experienced people like me. Nigel was planning a trip to the Alps with a couple of friends for a few days skiing, would I like to come? Having only just come back it would be a bit irresponsible to go again, though tempting. I really ought to be looking for a new job, so I said 'No'.

I was late again for school, although this time it was definitely not my fault. Gen's mother would insist upon his wearing two socks of the same colour, but as I hadn't got round to doing the laundry, I couldn't find two to meet this exacting specification, without either holes in the left sock, or Dennis the Menace on one and Ninja Turtles on the other. It was entirely her fault because she rejected my more pragmatic policy of buying job lots of identical socks so that they didn't have to be sorted out. All my own socks are charcoal grey.

'Cushy number you're on, then, all that money . . . in my day. . .' said Mr Gibbon as I passed him on the way to school. Trotsky growled in acquiescence. He must wait for me. I didn't stop to listen.

I cut the grass for the first time since October while I waited for the washing machine to finish its programme; it would take quite a lot more grooming before I could irritate Mr Gibbon by having more immaculate stripes on the lawn than his.

As I pushed the mower up and down, I thought things through. Although I had only worked precisely two days in the last twenty-five, I did need a little time away from distractions to consider my future before I really got stuck into the business of garnering gainful employ. I wasn't going to make market maker Ron's error of rushing into the first job I was offered. I rang Nigel (the redundant) and said 'Yes', and the headhunters and said 'The week after next'.

Rika could see two sides to the skiing argument. She was relieved that she didn't have to go – indeed was not invited – but I sensed she thought I should be looking for a job more actively. However, with me in my emasculated can't-even-support-his-own-family-shock-of-redundancy state she was sufficiently sensitive not to say anything.

I was losing track of time already.

On Sunday the darling spouse lay in while I gave the bairn his breakfast. The boys in her film crew were back from Venice (or was it Cannes?) for a bit of R&R in somewhere civilised. She had thus been out until three singing karaoke.

After breakfast Gen and I went to the weekly car boot sale. Gen acquired an 007 Aston Martin (Corgi c.1967 – I had one when I was a boy), pre-ejected passenger, sunroof etc. (twenty pence), I a folding camera (pre-war? Carl-Zeiss, Jena), something of a restoration project, but in its day clearly an item of quality (twelve pounds). And then we saw it.

'Daddy, buy that train.'

A big black monster with Union Pacific written on the side, it had at least thirty-six wheels and was magnificent. Pongo Parton gave away our train set when I was about three on being posted abroad. I had never forgiven him.

'Fifty pounds.'

'Forty,' I riposted.

'This retails at £170 new, mate.'

I looked at it, and I believed him. 'All right fifty then.' A tough bargain was struck. In situations like this I found my predatory City instincts useful.

There was no point in having a non-motive locomotive so we bought a transformer (five pounds), plus for Gen who would be allowed nowhere near my monster, half a dozen coaches (a pound each), a diesel shunter (six pounds), and a small steam engine (four pounds). We needed track, so the man sold us enough to go round the living room twice (three pounds), blackened with age, the electric points fused together by countless mini Chernobyls. The brand name Tri-ang struck a nostalgic chord.

Half an hour later the track was indeed going twice round the living room floor. Miraculously all the trains worked. It was difficult to know which boy was more excited – it certainly beat stockbroking. Mum came down for breakfast at about eleven. I made her some strong coffee. She looked at me and then at our trains, a glimmer of despair in her eyes.

It was nice to be free of the tyranny of the Sunday papers. I still bought them, but I read them for pleasure, and avoided the business pages.

I leafed indolently through the appointments section. I owed it to myself to look for jobs outside the City. 'Product Manager, Milton Keynes, Attractive Package.' I could imagine what that would be. About twenty-five grand, if that, and a Vauxhall Cavalier. The idea is that you are driven to greater things by your aspiration to drive a Vauxhall Carlton. I pictured myself in Vauxhall's TV ad; a smooth industrialist (which might be a contradiction in terms) with a touch of distinguished grey, enviously looking the other vehicles up and down in the company car park, and plotting the downfall of Jones in sales.

I reached for the colour supplement instead.

In the evening, Gen, who clearly loved his trains, couldn't be persuaded to eat supper or have his bath. Normally I had trouble getting him out of his bath. I eventually got him into bed with the promise of three Thomas the Tank Engine stories. He wanted to know why the toy train I had bought him was Number Six and not Number One and was red not blue. Taxed for an acceptable explanation I told him that it was Percy. Gen was lost in thought, but seemed satisfied, and went to sleep. My bluff would probably revisit me because I was dimly aware that Percy was the green engine.

It was getting on for a week in the awful predicament of being unemployed. The ghastliness of this was, I thought, overstated.

The advantages of unemployment were manifold and obvious:

1. Lie-in every day. (In theory – in practice give Gen his breakfast while wife lies in.)
2. The sun was shining.
3. I saw more of Gen (when Rory's parents allowed).
4. I got extra holiday I didn't expect, inc. skiing.
5. I could get the garden sorted out.
6. I could do all those DIY jobs I should have done two years ago on moving into this house.
7. I could get really good at the piano.

This last was a long-standing ambition. I had spent the golden hello Phillips and Drew gave me (the suckers, I was desperate to join them) on a stupendous black grand piano. It gave me a tremendous sense of power as it stretched in front of me, of the kind that other men derive from inordinately long zoom lenses or E-Type Jaguars. Gen wanted me to play 'The Snowman' but it was too difficult so I was currently learning 'Für Elise'.

I walked Gen up to school on time to general, if patronising, approval. There was only one other father, with lank, unkempt-looking hair and a nose ring. Obviously a workshy dole scrounger.

On the way back I met Mr Gibbon again, on the way to get his newspaper. I decided to come clean with him.

'I've been made redundant,' I said.

'That's terrible' he said, his eyes brightening considerably. Trotsky gave my shoes a friendly lick. 'Are you getting the dole, then? I was out of work for five years once. Of course in those days you didn't get much dole.'

The dole! Me! 'I don't think it's right for people like me to claim social security Mr Gibbon', I replied.

'Why not?' he asked before realising that the reason was that I was probably so rich that I didn't need to. He stopped looking so cheerful and dragged Trotsky into his house.

Later, I clean forgot to pick up Gen from school. The teacher was distinctly frosty because it meant that she had had to miss her lunch.

11

Nigel came round to pick me up. We were to meet his farmer friend and his accountant friend near Dover. We were cutting it a bit fine with regard to the ferry, but just as he arrived the phone rang.

It was my mother-in-law from Japan. Instead of saying that Rika was not in, I foolishly mentioned that I had lost my job.

'*Nani? Shitsugyo desu ka?*' (What? Lost your job?)

'*Hai.*' (Yes.)

'*Nippon dewa kangaerarenai.*' (In Japan, unthinkable.)

'Well here it has happened. Don't worry, I will soon get another one,' I said, eyeing my ski bags. The conversation was soon out of control. 'Anyway,' I said, 'I haven't got time to explain, I'm just off for an interview, right this minute, and I'm late. Goodbye.'

'That's not fair, Jim san, you have to explain.' In the background Nigel was thundering out 'Chopsticks' on the piano, and telling me to 'Hurry up with that Japanese crap'.

'I have explained,' I said, 'I've got no job.'

'But you can't have no job.'

'Well, I have got no job.'

' How can you have no job?'

The conversation was developing a certain circularity. 'Mother,' I said firmly, 'I have to go . . . for an interview . . . now.' Surely a cast iron excuse, even if it was a lie. '*Nan de isoide iru no? Dare ga piano hite iru no ka?*' (But you can't be in a hurry, who's playing the piano?)

'Nigel, stop playing the piano, you're undermining my case.'

'Well hurry up then, we're late for the ferry.'

'Why are you talking English?' said my mother-in-law. I knew from long experience that my mother-in-law when aroused, at all other times charming, was like a pit bull terrier. She wouldn't let go. I could guess she must be worrying that I would no longer be able to keep her daughter in the lavish manner to which she was accustomed.

'I really have to go now, I'm getting very late for my interview. Goodbye,' I said.

'What interview?'

I slammed the phone down, aware that slamming phones down on mothers-in-law is a capital offence in any country in the world, but skiing was more important.

On the way to Dover I posted the signed letter to Merrill Lynch accepting the redundancy payment offered to me.

We stopped off near Dover at Nigel's farmer friend's house. I never discovered his real name for sure, it might have been Giles, but his friends called him Wurzel. I wondered if he found this as irritating as I find being called Dolly, but he didn't seem to mind. And friends found the sobriquet 'Wurzel' hilarious, just as they found the sobriquet 'Dolly' hilarious.

The other friend, Basil, an accountant to high net worth individuals a.k.a. the filthy rich, had felt a need to cram in an extra morning's work so had saved time by coming to Dover by train separately. Basil's pay accrued by the quarter hour of advice, each such 'unit' being worth the redistribution of fifty pounds of wealth in his favour.

We missed the ferry by five minutes, thanks to my pit bull mother-in-law, so returned to the lovely farmhouse and drunk in the beauty of the Garden of England, while waiting for the next one. The weather was warm, summer beckoned.

Wurzel was bemoaning the stress of farming. Two stockbrokers and a City accountant looked at him as if he were mad. The Channel Tunnel had compulsorily bought some of his land, and it was taking longer than expected to sell off another bit for a planned motel near the new motorway, because of a group of anti-entrepreneurial lefties on the council. The caravan park on some European Community set-aside land hadn't been the roaring success he had originally anticipated either, and the C.A.P. beet subsidy was under threat. He was a Lloyds name. The pathos of it was too touching for words.

The record time down to the Cowshed is about seven and three quarter hours, achieved at the dead of night in my stockbroker mobile (Requiescat In Pace). The ten hours driving in a distinctly unsouped-up family mobile provided by Wurzel were dominated conversationally by Basil sorting out Wurzel's financial problems. 10 hours x 4 x £50 = £2,000 worth of free advice. On such trips, Radio Four fades depressingly near Calais.

He ate, drank, but sadly didn't sleep, accountancy. Accountancy is supposed to be dull, and Basil didn't exactly succeed in making it sound interesting, but I deeply envied his obvious enjoyment of his job. It was like being trapped for ten hours in a small space with an endless tape of the BBC 'Money Programme'. By the time we arrived he had created complicated trust funds neatly solving the problem of how to settle a quarter of a million on to Wurzel's toddler and his wife's foetus. The farm itself was to be transferred into the name of his foreign wife, which would somehow achieve a total avoidance of any Capital Gains taxes if his motel got planning permission and he sold off the land to a developer for a massive profit.

Wurzel looked worried at these suggestions. Personally, I would have killed for some of this stress.

The proposal might incur the wrath of the Revenue, which would be powerless to do anything about it, but in any case, Basil was scathing about the Inland Revenue; any decent tax inspector they had ever employed was soon poached by one of the big accountancy firms. The rotten tax inspectors spend their time trying to suck up to said accountancy firms to try to get a job. Deep down, these civil servants are all Thatcherite supporters of the private sector, Basil explained. It was the embittered NUPE members who'd failed to get a job in the private sector who were the danger.

Having a foreign wife too, I tackled him with my financial problems; 'Get an English one,' he said. About fifty pence's worth of free advice. Witty for an accountant.

At a service station halfway down the motorway, we bumped into a posse of Sloane Rangerette friends of Nigel's, with names like

Twiddles, Fluff and Zara, who were on their way to Courchevel. Before I knew it we were contracted to meet them there for dinner the following night, a plan imbued with sadness for me as Courchevel had associations of Alick going on about his bonus.

We broke the journey during the night in a pleasant one star hotel near Dijon, and arrived at the Cowshed at ten in the morning. Nigel already knew its reputation, because he was a friend of Alick's, despite also having been fired by him back in Swiss Bank Corp days.

Wurzel had heard from some gloom-monger that this part of the valley had lost virtually all its snow. I assured them that with my extensive local knowledge I would find some somewhere. I was still ski fit, and wanted to kick butt. I didn't want to end up renting the chalet next to Twiddles, Fluff and Zara in bloody Courchevel, and prevailed on the group to stay at the Cowshed.

I wrestled with stopcock G and system draining tap A. Having been occupied only two weeks before, the walls of the Cowshed were still warm, so there were no frozen pipes this time and with an all-male contingent there was no need to indulge in euphemisms about the delicacies of the plumbing. 'Should you get lucky, don't put your rubber johnnies down the loo.'

Fat chance. In five years of marriage I hadn't been propositioned once. Nigel, a balding bachelor, prematurely grey without being distinguished, and with a paunch, had the best chance, if he could get the girls sniffing that greatest of aphrodisiacs; money. (Like Wurzel and I, Basil was boringly, and as far as one could ascertain happily, married.)

We got to the slopes in time for the half day, and I found myself, Chip-like, agitating for a rapid ascent up the mountain. I was outvoted and we succumbed to the sixty-seven franc menu. Later we found enough snow to confound gloom-monger Wurzel, and had an excellent afternoon's skiing.

In the evening we slogged up to Courchevel so that Nigel could flaunt his wealth in front of Twiddles, Fluff and Zara. The meal came to twenty-five pounds a head, which he loudly proclaimed a huge bargain compared to a comparable meal in London, especially as Basil had chosen some Pouilly St Pseudy Wine Bore to accompany the pudding.

We passed an agreeable few days on the pistes. My purpose of unencumbered reflection upon my future in an environment of total relaxation was only achieved so far as the total relaxation; I didn't think about my future once. The team did a little bit of thinking on my behalf and advised me that I was unsuited to be a salesman.

Unpersuasive, easily dupable, unforceful character. How do people spot these things so quickly? I guess it's that every time I suggested something like 'Let's go skiing now,' or 'How about a slightly cheaper bottle of wine?' or 'Isn't it a waste of time to drive all the bloody way to Courchevel to flirt with Twiddles, Fluff and Zara when we have our own exciting company?' I was overruled. I couldn't sell my ideas.

Some of my ideas were right however. The expeditions to Courchevel had presented no threat to my father's plumbing: Nigel would only be earning eighty or ninety grand, enough to pay fifty pounds a head for a date, but with typical stockbroker's commitments like an overambitious mortgage, scarcely enough to impress these girls. Life is much more straightforward if you are born with money. Nigel should look for a nice girl from the East End.

We ate out locally a few times too, in places where prices are half what they were in the resorts, and the food better. Good honest country fair. The best things in life are not free, but they are cheap.

The only reason we managed to pay fifteen pounds a head is because Basil the wine buff insisted on buying good vintages from well-known vineyards. It seems bizarre to me to fork out more on a drink than on the meal itself. The interest in knowing about wine is obvious, but too much knowledge, once acquired, has risks. I would hate to lose my love of plonk.

I figured out a way of introducing plonk onto the table, in the guise of a few 'interesting local wines'. It was quite a good stratagem because although wine snobs can bullshit about Claret or Beaujolais, the Vins de Savoie are not heavily written up in the *Vogue Book of Wine*, so the likes of Basil are not quite sure what to say.

It was time to get back to the UK, and leave the mountains glinting invitingly in the sunlight. Nigel and I, the unemployed, agitated for another day's skiing, but sadly Wurzel had to tend to his lambing and his planning application, and Basil to the problems of the obscenely rich. For Basil, time really was money and fifty pound units were needlessly ticking away so we had no choice but to return.

For the first time in years I could have stayed on holiday, and yet I was returning. God, I must be a dull person. Returning to look for a job. How responsible.

The normal end of holiday 'Condemned Man Eats Hearty Breakfast' feeling was absent, but nonetheless, there was a sense of foreboding about knuckling down and seeking employment.

We broke the journey with a lovely meal in Beaune, in the heart of Beaujolais, where Basil loaded up on a case of needlessly expensive wine because 'It's so much cheaper than in England'. What's wrong with Safeway's Bulgarian Cabernet Sauvignon which is far cheaper? It must be the academic joy of avoiding taxes that appealed to his accountant's mind, because I still don't believe that Basil could tell a Burgundy from a Bordeaux except by the shape of the bottle.

It is a cliché, but like all clichés, contains truth; as we got to Reims, Calais began to appear on the signposts and it started to cloud over. By the turning off for Amiens the car was being buffeted by the wind, and by Calais it was raining. In Dover there was a knifing cold wind. When we had left England it had felt almost like summer.

We spent the night at Wurzel's outside Dover. I lay in until late (10 a.m.), so that by the time I got up, Basil had caught an early train in order not to miss out on the notching up of any more units than necessary. Living proof that it is possible to have a boring job and love it. Let's be quite honest about Basil. He is a bastard and I hate him. In a nice way; out of naked envy.

Wurzel was off attending to his lambing so Nigel and I went out to witness the agriculturalist's stress at first hand. The farm presented a happy scene. I found myself humming the theme tune to *The Archers*. There were ewes in the field waiting to lamb, and mothers suckling newborns indoors. There was the odd carcass dotted around; sheep apparently have a habit of dying for no good reason, so I could see the stressful side of farming, but despite the cold wind, I'd rather have worked there than in the City. Nigel agreed, except that he had a rather irritating way of putting it. 'I'd rather work here, but I suppose it's not too bad earning more than the Prime Minister.' I had only been earning more than the Chancellor.

I felt more positive again. I had a God-sent opportunity to sit back, pick and choose, and remedy that particular problem. (Merrill Lynch may not often get referred to as God, but I don't suppose they mind.)

12

Back at home the expected fat redundancy cheque had not appeared through the letter box. There was only a somewhat hostile letter demanding the return of the battered Vauxhall Astra a.s.a.p. and a statement to the effect that there would be no redundancy dosh for me until such time as it were given back. It could wait a day or so. I decided to waste a day at home rehabituating myself to my surroundings and psyching myself up to start the job hunt.

Rika was at home too, organising a film shoot on the telephone. She was not capable of having a short conversation on a telephone, which meant that my job hunting would have to be done in snatches, or from a public call box, or, perish the thought, by letter. In the City you do not get jobs by writing letters, and certainly not by filling in application forms, but through introductions from friends, direct telephone calls, followed by faxing the C.V. (often you can get away without doing this, and should unless the C.V. is a real humdinger), or through headhunters.

Personnel men are to be avoided like the plague.

Personnel men are quite commonly women; this balances up numbers a bit and allows a firm to claim that it is an 'equal opportunities employer'. Personnel people are the nearest you get to a civil servant in the City. Like people at the DTI, they use the word 'entrepreneur' a lot, without having the first idea what such a person might be. The personnel woman's role is to dot t's and cross i's on the actual contract. She is a mere functionary, stays a safe distance from executives such as self, is paid twenty-five grand – not bad compared to the rest of the populace – and kept happy with an important title like Director of Personnel. She, or her assistant, is usually being shagged by the Head of Bond Trading, whose salary she knows. She tries to get you to fill in application forms, but you ignore her, until employment terms have been agreed by the man who employed you.

If this description sounds outrageously sexist, it is not my fault; I merely record things as they are.

The only person in the personnel department who exerts real power is the company car man (male), who is universally held in fear and respect by everyone in the company. He collects parking fines more effectively than any policeman or bailiff because failure to do so affects his cost centre, and thus his bonus. He is probably the only true entrepreneur in the whole department, running scams with cars which ought not really to be insurance write-offs or doing deals with mates on the servicing 'to save costs'. Directing a million pounds worth of cars towards a particular garage has got to be worth a backhander or two.

A good relationship with the company car man can make the difference between an XR3i and a Porsche (if one has just become available because a bond trader has been 'let go'). He himself alternately drives a Daimler V12, and a Mercedes 500 SEL sports car, depending on whether he is trying to impress the mates down the golf club or some peroxide blonde with big boobs down the pub. He is the most powerful man in the firm.

Successive budgets have made the company car man an endangered species. It is still an advantage to be given a company car, but only just, and the advantage is one mainly of hassle free motoring, rather than money.

The Merrill Lynch man wanted his Astra back. I felt unlucky. I had hoped to be one of those who continued to drive their company cars for months on end after being fired. The personnel lady is usually jealous of the power of the company car man and often does not keep him up to date on the latest round of firings.

I went in to see my first headhunter.

The Dickensian-sounding Mr Crump kept me waiting forty-five whole minutes, which stretched the patience somewhat. As an erstwhile highly-paid, and soon to be even more highly-paid executive, I should not be kept waiting.

While waiting for Mr Crump, a young assistant chatted to me amicably. His name was Donald. 'Camberwell? Three bedroom house, in the Georgian part, you get some real bargains down there don't you? What? Bought it in 1989? Five years in the City, wife works in television, don't get paid much do they? Yes, we were thinking of sending our one there, nice school? Nice suntan, skiing? Interesting C.V., I think there will be a lot of demand for you. Merrill Lynch, yes, absolutely ruthless, great for turnover, we have quite a few people through here from there.'

He asked me all sorts of personal questions which seemed to be culled from a psychological assessment paper in the guise of 'getting down a few personal details'. By the end I think he had not only my age, sex, and experience, but a good idea of domestic outgoings, size of mortgage, wife's earnings, and a lot else besides. Bloody cheek! I suppose it was to gauge where he could slot me on the psychological assessment paper's greed rating, and thus what amount of commission I'd be likely to earn him. He would have discovered that I was still locked in a 1980s mindset, and considered myself worth more than the Prime Minister (well, as much as Nigel anyway).

Mr Crump asked me why I was made redundant and what my ambitions were. Tricky questions. I was made redundant because I was useless, and as for my ambitions, these were things with which my life so far had remained remarkably unencumbered, beyond a loose desire to earn lots of money whilst unencumbered with too much work or responsibility.

I said that I was in no hurry in my job hunt and wanted to take this opportunity to make sure that I got something worthwhile, that my next job was a good one, and also I wanted to look at the possibility of work outside the City altogether, because I understood that Mr Crump's outfit didn't specialise only in the City. I was quite keen to go abroad too, somewhere warm, Paris, Madrid, Milan, Hong Kong, Manila perhaps even Tokyo, with fat overseas allowances. I was very flexible and so was my wife, I told him, although I hadn't told her yet how flexible she was. In fact, I would consider anything although it would probably have to involve sales of some kind. Management was probably out, I mused. (Despite my salary I had somehow failed to become even Assistant Director at P & D, or Assistant Vice President at Merrills, a title dished out to virtually everyone with more than a few years' experience. At Merrills I had been a mere Financial Consultant.)

Any non-City job would probably have to be some kind of sales or marketing, I said, without having the first idea of the difference between the two. Marketing only existed in the City in firms with large bureaucracies, like UBS Phillips and Drew, with its philanthropic policy of providing employment for people called Ruedi.

'Do you know what people in industry earn?' I was asked abruptly.

'Well, no, not exactly, but I realise that it is less.'

'How much did you earn?'

'£65,000 a year,' a slight exaggeration, but I had decided to add on £5,000, and then make myself believe the lie so that I didn't make any slip-ups, for negotiation purposes.

'A good widget seller earns £20,000 a year. A top widget seller makes £30,000 a year, maybe a bit more. You have no experience of widgets.' The widget is a generic term for all industrial products. 'Who will pay you anything like what you need? What's more, you might have to live in Manchester.'

He treated me like a little boy, and as for what I needed, I think that he was assuming too much. What I 'needed' was a difficult concept. Did I really 'need' £1,500 a month left after mortgage, overdraft, gas and electricity, £1,000 after Rika's phone bill?

'I am afraid that I cannot recommend your candidature to my clients when you don't even know what you want to do yourself. Come back when you are serious.'

This high-handed, dismissive attitude was unexpected. Headhunters should be sycophantic and ingratiating. 'Pleased to be of service,' they are supposed to lisp. In the City evolutionary scale they come quite a long way below stockbrokers for slime and scale. If we brokers are reptiles, then headhunters are bicuspid molluscs.

They exist because City firms don't like to be seen to be ungentlemanly. The dirty work of poaching talented members of the opposition gets sub-contracted. A bit like murder in the Mafia. For their pains the headhunters get around a third of the first year's salary as a fee, which isn't bad.

Stockbrokers can argue that their function in society is to lubricate the wheels of commerce by directing money towards efficient companies through the medium of high share prices for the good, and low ones for the bad. We are an essential for the good of society. Headhunters too have a function, in their capacity of bicuspid molluscs. As the reptile stockbrokers swim overhead crapping, the headhunters feed on the waste below, cleaning it up. The ecology of the City would collapse without its molluscs, just like any other swamp.

At this point I should mention that some of my best friends are headhunters. The Bloomsbury Group's Mr Christopher Lawless has been especially helpful to me in the past, getting me my first two jobs. I feel thoroughly disloyal ever to have been near Mr Crump's office. Sorry, Chris.

I had been kept waiting for forty-five minutes, then told not to waste the irascible Mr Crump's time. The indignity of it. To torture my metaphor further, we reptile brokers were dinosaurs turning to each other and asking 'Hey, did you hear that?' (if you accept the current theory that dinosaurs were wiped out by a massive meteor thudding into the Earth and causing the equivalent of a nuclear winter). There was quite a lot of crap and decaying dinosaur to be cleared up in the aftermath of the Big Bang and the 1987 crash. It was the age of the mollusc scrabbling around for unwholesome detritus, not exactly nutritious enough to help them evolve backbones, but enough to keep them going.

* * *

On my way home I needed to calm my anger, so I decided to seek relief by purchasing one of those magazines with a glossy cover; the sort that one requests to have dropped into an anonymous brown paper bag, or which one receives mail order. Before slipping into my fantasy world, I made sure that the wife was out. My heartbeat began to pick up fractionally as I unpeeled the wrapping in a room with suitably subdued lighting. *Railway Modeller's Monthly.*

It was time to consider how to permanently assemble all the components I had bought at the car boot sale. Here at last was a text that would unravel for me the secrets of OO gauge as compared to HO gauge, and explain to me the very best method of constructing papier-mâché mountains, box girder bridges, and getting realistic grass or bushes on the Alpine meadows I'd planned, or authentic-looking tarmac on the road leading up to the main station, for Gen's cars.

My pulse picked up as I looked through the table of contents. 'GUTTERING IN 2MM SCALE' by Bert Stafferton, and 'BRINKWORTH GOODS SHED REVISITED' by Harry Middle. 'When Mike Barclay dropped round, and said, "Harry, we need a model of a pre-war G.W.R. engine shed, and we need it quick," I was only too happy to search through my box of 4mm scale purlins and trusses and see what I could come up with . . . I copied the method Nick Cant used in building a Midland coaling stage, described in *Railway Modeller's Journal* April 1967 . . .'

I read on enthralled, if a little intimidated at the standards required. Perhaps a model of the London Underground would be better. Then no one could argue about authenticity, because it could legitimately run in the dark, and never be seen.

13

The job hunt had to start in earnest. I think it was lucky that it was now May and the skiing season was definitively over. I might have been tempted to go and do some more 'thinking over' in France.

Rika would soon be vacating the telephone for a week or so. There was no excuse. Sod the train set, sod the garden; on yer bike, Jim. A man has to get a job.

She was off to a television trade conference in Cannes (or was it Venice?). She would be manning the Japanese stand designed to sell the Japanese standard as the world's next broadcasting standard, i.e. for High Definition TV. It is all part of an overall strategy for total world domination. HDTV is amazing, the picture quality is better than a glossy magazine, and we will all want it, there is no question. Rika would be there to help ensure that it was the Japanese who supplied it, as they will, of course, because the Europeans, led by the French, are about five years behind with their standard. (NB: This para was written in 1991; so far – 1994 – HDTV is a flop; its day will come, but the US standard looks like being adopted worldwide.)

* * *

Nigel had suggested that I call his old employers who had fired him, as he would need replacing. I gave a man with a funny Eurotrash sounding name at Paribas, a call.

I began to explain my situation; 'Merrill Lynch, well you know how the Americans are, decided to let me go, not very long term. I talk to the Japanese about European markets, and I gather you might be looking for some new salesmen.'

Nigel was not a contact to mention, his own departure having been somewhat less than voluntary, although technically he had resigned.

'Absolutely no interest,' he replied, a little harshly for the good of my feelings it seemed to me. As a salesman I had no right to be disconcerted. Cold calling new clients was something like this. Never pleasant. I pressed on with my patter until he managed to get rid of me with 'Send in your C.V. and I promise to look at it.' This was unlikely to mean that I had got my salesman's foot in the door. It meant 'Don't call me, I'll call you,' or less politely, 'Bugger off'.

Imagine my surprise, therefore, when ten minutes later Rika – not yet in Venice (or was it Cannes?) – passed me the phone. 'It's for you,' she said somewhat crossly, as if I had no right to use it. It was a strange attitude. Didn't she realise that an employed Jim meant a Jim not competing for the telephone? Didn't she also realise, more importantly, that her Japanese love of consumer undurables with brand names like Louis Vuitton was threatened by my continued lack of absurdly remunerative employment? Women are strange creatures. I don't understand them.

The call was from Mr Crump's assistant, Donald. They had a client looking for experienced European salesmen and might be able to fix an interview. The man with the Eurotrash name from Paribas. This man could have had the chance to save the thirty per cent of my first year's salary that would go in fees to Mr Crump. He'd had me on the phone only fifteen minutes earlier. What an idle bastard. Pay at Paribas was obviously not linked to costs. I liked the sound of the place. I agreed to go in to see him the next day.

'Are you back at work, then, Mr Parton?' said Mr Gibbon, over the garden fence, Trotsky gnashing at his side. At least Mr Gibbon calls me 'Mr Parton'. He is too old to have heard of Dolly.

'No, just an interview, I'm going to play the field a bit, before making a decision.' Mr Gibbon and Trotsky snorted in unison and disappeared back into his house.

I planned the interview carefully. I had to be a bit wary, because the last thing I wanted was to be offered a job immediately. First I had to suss the market, then ideally bring the whole process to the boil with three firms offering me jobs simultaneously. I could then play one off against the other. On no account, I resolved, would I mention my secret desire to get into widgets. I would play slightly hard to get, but act as if the City was under my skin and in my blood.

'Why were you made redundant, Mr Parton?' A tricky question. I assumed that Mr Crump wouldn't have explained the real reason; he'd have been undermining the sales pitch he must have made on my behalf if he had. I wasn't about to admit to low commission numbers either: candour about my business prospects in the face of an inquisition by Alick's boss at Merrill Lynch had cost me my job.

I talked about the long term. 'My chosen client base, the Japanese, are a bit short of cash at the moment, but on a five-year view they will of course come bouncing back; the Wall of Money will return; it will only be necessary to achieve a minute market share to make the whole business fabulously profitable. Take my client Nomura Investment Trust Management, they have more money under management than the entire Japanese defence budget, and the Japanese Army is the eighth largest in the world. You pick up a tenth of a per cent of that business, and . . . wow.'

They had given me the biggest order I ever got, worth £6.8 million, not bad, but my biggest ever. It was the biggest order I got by a multiple of about six. Most brokers will be unimpressed.

The Eurotrash man's eyes were already glazed over.

I had made a fatal mistake with the first thing I had said; I had mentioned the long term. If stockbrokers think you can make loads of money for them quickly they will employ you, and if they don't, they won't. At all costs, in an interview, the long and short term should be confused. For God's sake don't tell them it will take five years.

For the rest of the interview we went through the motions.

'Why do you prefer dealing in the French market to the Italian market?'

'There is better liquidity in France,' I answered, referring not to the ease of dealing, but to the booze. Real answer: 'I am being interviewed by a French firm.' (The real answer was not all that clever; Paribas Securities in London was independent and had little to do with France.)

The Eurotrash man was not one for too many excess motions. He was polite enough to ask me a few more questions but wrapped things up pretty quickly. The interview didn't last more than fifteen minutes.

As we parted he said, 'I'll be in touch'. I knew he was lying. He probably wouldn't even call the headhunter to say 'Who was that lemon you sent me? Do better next time.'

It was a pity, Paribas's offices are in the West End which would have made a pleasant change from the City. Very near the Steinway and Bösendorfer studios. My Yamaha grand is not really like a Jaguar E-Type. More like owning a three litre Nissan ZX sports car. Really I wanted an Aston Martin, in piano terms, a Bösendorfer.

Oh well, one interview down, fourteen to go. I had worked out that there were approximately fifteen jobs suitable for me in the City, which would use my skills and experience properly. If I failed on those I would have to lower my aim, and perhaps even become a widget salesman.

I learnt another lesson from this interview; if it is all over very quickly, or in other ways goes badly, kill time in a book shop before going home.

'That was quick,' said Rika, as I walked in through the front door, using a tone of voice reserved for the same words used in a different context about a different entrance. Talk about kicking a man when he is down.

That evening I drove her to the airport for her Cannes trip. (Or was it Venice?)

Mr Crump's assistant Donald phoned the next day to ascertain what the prognosis was for picking up his fee. There was no need to spare him the truth, it had been a disaster.

A succession of other headhunters telephoned me over the next few days. The news had got around that Jim Parton was available. They were like bees buzzing round a thimble of honey: headhunters too had been struggling, so a thimble of honey was better than none. Although Mr Crump had treated me somewhat arrogantly, because he knew, and I was discovering, that I was in a weaker position than I imagined, things weren't great for him either. Bullied people often become bullies.

Financial institutions were no longer expanding in the way they had in the 1980s. Many people would have been easy to lure into a greedy decision to upgrade their pay by changing employers a couple of years earlier, but were now conscious of job security perhaps being worth as much as a crazy salary. The accounting term Last In First Out, LIFO, was on everyone's lips. Not many would shift jobs for fear of being LIFOed. Gone were the days when headhunters could move an entire four-man analyst team to Morgan Stanley at average salaries in excess of £100,000 and pick up a fee of 30% x £100,000 x 4 = £120,000 just for setting up a few interviews, which were bound to succeed.

Most headhunters were suitably ingratiating. For the sake of narrative simplicity I will call them all Donald and treat them as if they were all the same person, which they may as well have been, with the exception of Mr Crump, and of course my excellent friends at the Bloomsbury Group.

Donald had a suitably ingratiating inflection in his voice. 'Hi Jim, how are things with you?' There would be a hint of infectious chuckle built into the 'Hi' so that you'd get the impression that the act of talking to you had improved his whole day. Not dissimilar to my broking technique.

I'd go into Donald's office. Typically Donald would be an ex-Army officer who had made it into the City, but through ignorance or mischance had ended up helping others earn a fortune rather than earning one himself, like ex-Guards officers Alick and Henry. He wasn't so professional that he'd worry about presenting an unsuitable candidate to his client as Mr Crump had done. Come to that, when the chips were down Mr Crump had presented me to Paribas even though he said he wouldn't present me to anyone until I knew what I wanted. Times must have been hard.

Donald would come up with the same list of fifteen suitable jobs that I had come up with myself, plus a few unsuitable ones that I hadn't thought of because they weren't suitable. I'm a sucker for an interview, however, so I would generally agree to any proposal, such as meetings with small start-up brokers describing themselves as 'research boutiques', a euphemism for not having many analysts, without necessarily promising better research. Perhaps I am being a touch hard on these research boutiques, but to resurrect my reptile metaphor, they can perhaps be likened to the small, furry, warm-blooded creatures – er, rats – that in the long term have done rather well, whereas not a few Tyrannosaurus Rexes have gone, or are going, the way of Tyrannosaurus Rex. (UBS Phillips and Drew is more of a Brontosaurus although I wouldn't care to predict extinction for T. Rex Merrill Lynch.)

Rory's Mum had heard of my plight so we were invited to dinner again. A genuine victim of the recession would create a talking point. Her husband's company had recently laid off some mergers and acquisitions lawyers, so she said she knew what it was like. He himself was an insolvency lawyer, and thus having a rather good time of things.

Rory's Mum had invited the usual assortment of doctors, teachers and artists to provide balance to blatant, card carrying, pig-dog, greedy capitalists such as self, and her hanging-is-too-good-for-them husband. When asked what I did for a living, I found myself not quite able, in public, at least, to admit 'nothing'.

'I am an investment banker,' I said.

'Oh, how interesting,' said the lady sitting next to me.

'I have a cousin who's only twenty-six and he is a director of S.G. Warburg. Who do you work for?'

'For nobody.'

'Do you work for yourself? How enterprising.'

I found the lady irritating. I thought it would be fun to embarrass her. 'No, I was made redundant last week.'

The silence that followed was indeed an embarrassed one. I imagine you'd get a similar reaction by telling someone you have AIDS and only three months to live; redundancy was politically correct, but nonetheless embarrassing, certainly at that early stage of the recession.

To fill in the silence, my interlocutor said, 'There's been a lot of that in the City recently hasn't there? Were you one of a whole lot of people?'

'No,' I replied, 'I was the only one.'

Another awkward silence, then, 'I guess it was a question of Last In First Out? Ha, Ha, LIFO!'

'No, I wasn't making very much commission, so they fired me and have hired somebody new to replace me.' Which was true – Giussi, the beginner, was already doing far better than I had been, and in addition to Giussi, there was the new Nordic bandit, hired to open up the frozen North, my efforts directed at the Far East having proved that little bit too long term. 'You're looking very healthy on it, where did you get that suntan?' She attempted to steer the conversation off into safer realms.

'I have a lot of time on my hands at the moment, as you can imagine, so I try to take my mind off things by doing a bit in the garden.' Really it was a skiing suntan, but it was fun embarrassing further someone embarrassed at my misfortune.

'How much did they pay you off?' asked Rory's Dad. I indicated to him the amount in months, rather than figures, because I knew that what he really wanted to know was how much I earned (for the nosy – my pay off was about £10,000). 'Is that all?' he said. 'They should pay you lots more than that. They poached you from Phillips and Drew, didn't they? That means they persuaded you to leave a secure job where you were doing well, for an insecure one. I think you should sue them.'

He offered to do it for me. I took a bit of persuading, because I thought it could backfire on me. It wouldn't do to be preceded by a reputation for litigiousness in my quest for a job. In the City, *verbum est meum pactum*, my word is my bond.

On the other hand, just as being fired by Merrill Lynch could never be held against anyone, suing Merrill Lynch would scarcely be seen as infringing any code of decent behaviour or of honour. They extracted what they could from their employees (nothing in my case), and would expect their ex-employees to extract as much from them as possible (probably nothing, in my case). However, there was also the factor that they had been indecently decent about the redundancy money they had offered saying, 'We don't have to give you anything, James,' which had struck me as uncharacteristically altruistic at the time, and made me suspicious that I could have asked for more.

'Go for it,' I said. There was nothing to lose.

My resolve was further strengthened by the arrival of another letter demanding the return of the company car, or else no redundancy payment. In addition, it requested that I pay an outstanding parking fine.

14

A few days on, Donald rang. 'Hi, Jim,' he said with that laughing inflection of his. He had arranged an interview at the broking arm of a small merchant bank.

We were now several weeks into redundancy, and the garden was beginning to look considerably tidier, the train set was settling down into a layout involving tunnels, Alpine pastures, turntables, a viaduct, and a big station with a through line for passenger trains and sidings for shunting goods. Quite soon I would feel confident enough to start nailing the track to the baseboards. My piano playing was also giving me lots of pleasure, even if painful to all around.

Life was all rather pleasant. Sod it – who wanted to work anyway?

Donald's interview was thus something of an imposition; I would have to tear myself away from a busy round of weeding, get on a number thirty-five bus and go into the City. It would be a rude interruption because the company concerned was small, a boutique, but as Rika was hovering over me as I took her telephone at the time, back from Venice (or was it Cannes?) and dreaming Hermès (or was it Armani?), I had little choice but to accept.

I arrived about ten minutes late, which didn't matter especially, as the opposite side are always twenty minutes late.

Donald had told me who I was to see, but I was buggered if I could remember. Suzanna something. 'I've come to see the head of research, Suzanna . . .' I bluffed at reception. The surname Rosewall was supplied.

Ms Rosewall was rather alluring. My eyes glided involuntarily down to the fourth finger of her left hand, a part of the anatomy that should have had no interest for me, a married man, albeit to a predominately absentee wife. There was a huge rock thereon, which was probably just as well. I had never come close to an extra-marital liaison in my life, but as the former President Jimmy Carter used to say, I have frequently sinned in my heart.

We ran through my life history. A colleague came in and started telling me all about himself, and the firm, which is standard in an interview. The last thing anyone discovers is anything worth knowing about the candidate.

'We work on low basic salaries,' (= poverty), 'with a large commission share,' (= pressure). I could feel my enthusiasm for the job waning.

Ms Rosewall on the other hand was decidedly *comme il faut*, with her deep swimming-pool eyes, and blonde hair playing carelessly on sculpted shoulders of the heave in ecstasy variety. The nose was slightly squiffy, but with legs like that, who cared.

'What do you understand by return on capital?' she suddenly asked.

This was a faster, straighter ball than most. Return on capital was a fairly crucial concept for a stockbroker to grasp but I certainly didn't expect to be tested on it, or indeed anything else. We were there to establish what a good chap I was, not test me on my knowledge. That should be taken as read. A bloody career woman; Mrs Thatcher too was said to have been a bit of a stunner in her youth. Only two of the five companies I had worked for in the City had ever tested my assertion that my Japanese was fluent. Usually it went: 'You speak fluent Japanese? Here have a job.' Indeed, back in 1986, with the Japanese bull market in full swing, it was, 'You can handle a pair of chopsticks? Here have a job.'

In these hard times, employers were taking more care. Return on capital. Tricky, I thought. I had a rough idea of what is meant by this measure, having done several stock exchange accountancy courses (chiefly as a means of getting a break from the office), but had usually ducked the actual exams. Curiously, none of the employers who sent me on these courses ever checked on whether I had passed the exam, and in fact I did fail one or two. Any boss worth his salt ought to have splattered me against the ceiling for my indolence, but I never worked for that sort.

'Return on capital,' I looked at her as if she were mad. 'Well, it's quite straightforward, it's the return you get on the capital you invest, but obviously there are different ways of measuring it, I could talk about it for half an hour, if you wanted.' She looked impressed and my bluff was not called, possibly because I had called hers.

The job they had in mind for me was to talk to UK clients, something I had never done before. I didn't like the idea of working on a low salary for a high commission share, selling to sophisticated Brits, it sounded far too stressful. Sophistication implied that they would want to know the answer to the question 'What is the return on capital?' I could read this easily off the research prepared by the analyst, but I would have to understand how it was calculated, and how it compared with similar companies.

At the end of the meeting it was left that I would get back in touch if I was interested and at that time more serious discussions would take place. I didn't think I'd be calling.

Two jobs down, thirteen to go.

I had promised myself that I would investigate alternative, more lowly-paid careers in widget sales or whatever, but when the crunch came, I couldn't be bothered. My previous experience of interviewing for industrial jobs was that industrialists were most careful about whom they employed. I doubt very much that they are any better at selecting, but all that hassle of filling in long application forms, fighting onto a shortlist, winning through at the twenty-fifth attempt – after all I had no experience – was going to be a large effort for a low return. If British industry wants to attract bright people (and I don't mean me) they ought to remove some of the bureaucracy and career structures. The City gobbled up people in the 1980s, and still does, not just because of the money, but because there was a genuine chance of real responsibility within a couple of years for anyone, from any background.

But, as Nigel had said, you're better off with the job you know, and being paid more than the Prime Minister ain't all bad, or even a minor functionary like the Chancellor of the Exchequer. I was not about to approach the widget makers with missionary zeal and put them right; British industry has been in decline for a hundred years, and I would stick to what I knew. The job of Chancellor, we all know, is a stepping stone to greater things in the City. Nigel Lawson resigned just in time to get out of the way of the shit hitting the fan. Mr Major had a lucky escape from the most thankless task in politics, the shit subsequently splattering all over Mr Lamont.

The best government would be one that spent hours debating motorway bypasses round Twyford Down, or Maastricht, or the NHS, or evacuating Bosnian refugees; the less time available for thinking about the economy, the better. It is far too complicated for politicians, and should be left alone.

I had a series of interviews with City firms. Interviews definitely needed more planning and thought than they had as little as a year before, as I had discovered with the question on return on capital.

Quite a lot of the interviews were a complete waste of time. The opposition's purpose was to gather market intelligence. All had noticed a sharp drop off in Japanese commissions, indeed the business had never fulfilled the promise it had seemed to show only a couple of years before. The Japanese were not putting money abroad into shares. I could supply corroboration of the dawning perception that the Japanese as an investment power, certainly in equities, were in deep trouble.

At one leading merchant bank's broking subsidiary, the salesman, when his boss was out of the room, plaintively asked my advice as to whether he should chuck in the Japanese clients and move on to something else. He had a wife with a new baby to support, was probably feeling the pinch with the mortgage, and was worried by the lack of business. I wasn't about to tell him that I thought the Japanese were doomed, because it would have made him more determined to protect his patch and obstruct any suggestions of employing new people to attack his own client base, so I reassured him that he should stick it out for the long term. The Wall of Money might be delayed, but it would come. When British investment institutions started investing abroad the norm was to put ten per cent or so of funds abroad. That has more than doubled. The Japanese have yet to get as far even as ten per cent, I pointed out. I was looking for a job along his side. How could I tell him otherwise?

For whatever reason, I didn't get the job.

He also told me that before I left UBS Phillips and Drew, he and his colleague had been interviewing for a job there selling European equities to the Japanese, i.e. my job.

When I had been there you had had to be uniquely incompetent to be for the chop. My escape to Merrill Lynch had been very timely. Even if it had been only a temporary reprieve, it had been a lucrative one. Still, it is difficult to believe that P & D would have actually dispensed with me. I might not have been good, but there were worse, and many continue to have jobs there.

I ran up quite a large telephone bill talking to companies in Tokyo to try to get a job out there. A few years previously they would have fallen over themselves to employ me.

I had taught English in Japan for three years after university, and as my time came to an end I had an interview with Christopher Heath, the head of Baring Securities, which subsequently became the top foreign broking house in Tokyo, with Heath getting into the headlines as the highest-paid man in Britain, earning something in excess of two million pounds a year.

After a preliminary meeting over a drink with Heath, during which he told me to become a journalist, I was interviewed by someone called Richard Greer. I put him at about twenty-eight or so, frighteningly successful-looking, charming, but of a colourless, grey demeanour like a plant that has grown up under a flowerpot. He was interviewing me at 6.30 p.m., a time I considered that he should be at home or in the pub. He looked like a walking warning that stockbroking is damaging to your health. This one experience had pushed me towards returning to live in the UK, although I had sufficiently forgotten the shock of meeting him, it was not severe enough to prevent me from seeking employment in the City when I did return.

I had some interviews outside the City, with Shell for example, but they would have sent me on a two-year training course, followed by two years' work experience, by which time I would have forgotten my Japanese (I married Rika later). In the City I could use it immediately. It is this immediacy which makes British industry lose out to the City.

I accepted a job at Laurence Prust, who have since been closed down. They were such nice people, which is probably why. The deciding factor had been that at the second interview their Colonel Arthur had lavished lunch on me. At the time I was easily impressed by such things. At the third interview he had plied me with two or three pints, a bottle of wine and a couple of large glasses of port.

There had been no ugly talk of contracts and human resources departments. It was good old-fashioned 'my word is my bond' sort of place, which is how the City always used to operate. How could I say no?

My friend Chris Lawless, the headhunter, had also got a bond dealing outfit keen on me, but I decided that Laurence Prust were nicer, and that equities were more intrinsically interesting than bonds, which are all about interest rates, as opposed to companies making things either well or badly. Had Chris told me what he told me later, namely that the bond men would have paid me a starting salary of £20,000 (a large sum in 1986), I certainly would not have based my career path on the niceness of the people I was to work for.

Laurence Prust were gentleman stockbrokers in the old, and had one known it, rapidly disappearing mould. I joined six months or so before the Big Bang, when a change in the law meant that banks could own brokers, and jobbers. I found a far clearer explanation of the difference between brokers and jobbers than I can myself manage in the 1911 edition of *Nelson's Encyclopaedia*, one of my finest car boot sale acquisitions.

[Stock Exchange] members are divided into two classes – brokers and jobbers. The broker is he who transacts the business for the public, charging commission as agent. The jobbers are supposed to have no outside clients, but to confine their dealings entirely to brokers, to who they act the part of principles. Each jobber confines himself to certain classes of stocks and shares, and quotes his prices at such figures as to give him a fair chance of a making profit whichever way he deals. For example, he would quote a price of 97 11/16 to 97 13/16 – i.e. he is prepared to buy at 97 11/16 and to sell at 97 13/16.

I am one of the last ever Blue Buttons, the lowest of the low on the Stock Exchange floor, where share prices were made, and deals struck. With Big Bang, this method continued for a little while, but soon died in favour of doing it all on screens. A similar system continues at the New York Stock Exchange, where it now looks rather quaint.

A humble Blue Button could ask prices, but was not allowed to deal. I think you needed a silver button for that, I forget.

The barrow boy stock jobbers would see me coming and, detecting a certain polite public school nervousness, say the price so quickly I'd have to ask for it again. And again. They'd miss out the 'big number' so a share price of five pounds sixty seven was expressed as 'sixty-seven'. You were expected to know the 'five' bit. At least, post decimalisation, I didn't have to cope with sixteenths.

The worst thing was sitting first thing in the morning in the Laurence Prust 'box', a broom cupboard of an office, and listening to a jobber read off thirty prices, minus the 'big number' of course, at breakneck speed, and without saying which share they referred to. You were supposed to intuit that. Having missed half of them you were faced with the dilemma of admitting as much to your colleagues, or ringing the jobber back to hear them again, and enduring their impatient mockery.

The people at Laurence Prust were essentially kind, though. This was evident about six months later when Rika, my girlfriend from Japan, who had timed her study year in England to coincide with my return, had a small slip-up. My boss arranged a 'business trip' to Tokyo for me so that I could inform my future parents-in-law that they were shortly to be grandparents, and, worse, have a white man as a son-in-law. Being Koreans, they would have been pretty pissed off even if I'd been Japanese so they were somewhat less than thrilled about this prospect. Add in my own parents' reaction, and there's material there for a whole East meets West novel. I have a particular memory of being chased around the kitchen with a sushi knife (Japanese blades are the sharpest in the world) by my future father-in-law. For prudence's sake I ran off down the street in my socks, because there had been no time to grab my shoes from the footwell by the front door. Rika ran with me. The neighbours affected to take no notice, whereas in England, a small crowd might have gathered – in Korea too, for that matter. I don't think I was ever in serious danger as her father was not the most co-ordinated of men. At any rate, we survived to return to London, where Gen was born.

Strapped for cash, I stabbed my kind employers in the back, they who had paid my airfare to Japan. (If you are reading this, Mr Starr, and Colonel Arthur I still feel bad about it. Please call for your bottles of whiskey. It was a boy.) I left them for more money at Vickers da Costa, who never bothered to test my 'fluent Japanese'. Another decent company destroyed by the foreign bank who owned it. It still exists, vestigially. Against all the odds, some of the Japanese warrant people in my department have resisted blandishments to move to other firms and still work for something called Citicorp Scrimgeour Vickers. I think I know why, but it would be damn hard to prove in a libel court.

15

Confronted with acres of free time, it was easy to fall into the trap of doing absolutely nothing for entire days on end, except that I didn't regard it as a trap; it was rather pleasant. Being unemployed in London was certainly better than being from Nagorno Karabakh, or the marshlands in Southern Iraq, or Bosnia Herzegovina.

I wrote myself a long list of DIY tasks. The first of which would be to take up the old carpets, hire a floor stripper and sand the floor.

My piano playing was coming along well too. It was the first time that I had had the time to lavish as much attention as I desired on my E-type Jaguar substitute. 'Für Elise' was almost mastered, and I was embarking on 'The Entertainer'.

Mr Gibbon came round to complain that he could hear every note in every room in his house. Did I always have to play the same bloody tune? Apart from a right to make a noise in my own house, I would have thought that I had a right to expect a man of his age to be hard of hearing. Also, I could have said a thing or two about Trotsky, who would lean over the wall to bark at me every time I approached my own front door, and about Mrs Gibbon's six champion poodles, which I had never seen, but which I had certainly heard.

Mr Gibbon was full of surprises. He had played the trombone in the London Symphony Orchestra before the war, under such grandees of British music as Ralph Vaughan Williams, who had asked him technical questions about the instrument, for which he was writing a concerto. After the war, where a heart flutter had stopped him from fighting so he'd been sent down the mines, Mr Gibbon had not gone back into music, but into union politics. You would think that he might be in favour of my taking up playing the piano. His acute musician's ears, however, were very sensitive to all the noises emanating from my house, while apparently immune to those coming from his own. Now, a dog's barking was his music.

Trotsky was confined to the front yard, whilst Mrs Gibson's six show poodles had the run of the back. Any noise in our house, a slamming door or a creaking window, was greeted by barks in stereo; gruff and aggressive at the front, high pitched and yappy at the rear.

I had a secret desire to 'liberate' Trotsky into the back. Even if there were no bitches, to give the poodles an encounter with Trotsky would still be doing them a favour.

My Japanese mother-in-law had a Yorkshire terrier called Jack, no doubt a descendant of a small number of imported animals, because he was clearly inbred. Jack died recently, aged about seven. This was the most positive thing he had done in his short wretched life. Inbreeding had left him neurotic, incontinent, and only able to breathe in bronchitic wheezes. I had longed to release him back to where he belonged, taking on fifty rats in a ring while a dozen yokels bet on how many he could finish off in the allotted time.

(The new Crown Princess of Japan has a Yorkshire terrier called Chocolat. I suppose that if the dynasty has already survived two millennia, it may survive the foolishness of owning an inbred Yorkshire terrier, but one has to worry.)

I hope that Jack has found peace in death, and I can't help thinking that the six show poodles would benefit from the same. There was something that appealed to my sense of charity and goodness about the idea of Trotsky trotting around the backyard with a couple of poodles' windpipes in his mouth.

Not only was Mr Gibbon the ex-trombonist keeper of a fierce dog, he also had two wives, one upstairs, one down. When he divorced his first wife, an equitable financial settlement had not been possible, I suppose, so he had converted the upstairs into a flat for the original wife and lived downstairs with the new one.

The back garden had been divided in two with half given over to his first wife. The division was created with a sort of Berlin Wall down the middle. On one side the poodles painted slogans. This side had been concreted in to allow the second wife to hose it down after a good day's crapping by the poodles.

Mr Gibbon was a compulsive DIY fanatic. He could still wield a hammer even if no longer a trombone. He was continuously taking delivery of building materials, and having finished his Berlin Wall in the back garden and concreted over half the lawn, was constructing poodle powdering bays in new sheds. Very soon there would be no garden left, which was something to look forward to. I wondered if there were any more ex-wives under the concrete.

Occasionally, one caught a glimpse of the older Mrs Gibbon hanging some bloomers on her washing line. By the look of her she was about the same age as Mr Gibbon, around eighty, whereas the younger Mrs Gibbon was, relatively speaking, something of a floozy, being in her early seventies. Being a gentleman, I would never share my theories as to what her attractions were to Mr Gibbon, except to say that there was the odd visual clue available to neighbours on her washing line.

Seeing Mr Gibbon hard at work on his sheds I felt inspired to get myself organised to strip the old carpet and varnish the floorboards. I chose a time for this operation when Rika was still in Cannes (or was it Venice?) because I knew it would be fairly noxious, dirty work.

Removing the carpets had been Rika's idea. In Britain, we wear our shoes indoors, which is disgusting. Sensibly, the Japanese take them off. Thousands of congealed dog turds, or portions thereof, find their way onto Britain's Axminsters everyday, if you think about it. I deal with this by not thinking about it. I am too lazy to take my shoes off every time I go inside.

Rika has an obsession with dust, ascribing to it the cause of most illnesses. She could have employed a cleaning lady, but found English cleaning ladies too dirty and slapdash. This paradoxically led to us living in complete squalor, as she was not herself heavily into physical labour. I did a little cleaning but I preferred the creative side of things, making food for example, as opposed to clearing up afterwards.

I was often asked about cultural differences dividing my wife and I, and dirt was one. In Japan, if you leave a saucepan to 'soak' overnight because you can't be bothered to wash it, by morning there will be a trail of ants, and half a dozen cockroaches having a party on it. Outside of National Health Service hospitals, I don't think I've ever heard of a cockroach in England. They are extremely rare. There is no doubt that the English are dirtier than the Japanese because they can afford to be. I reject any suggestion that cleanliness is either genetically or culturally encoded. It is a function of climate. When it doesn't matter, the Japanese are amongst the filthiest people in the world. The Lake District in Britain is kept clean by visitors. Mount Fuji is strewn with litter. So are the Japanese beaches. And when the snow melts, a denser carpet of cigarette ends you could scarcely imagine than under Japanese chairlifts.

A people beset with contrasts, Rika once quoted at me rather a good Japanese proverb: 'You don't get good food out of a clean kitchen.' I thoroughly agree. A sterile kitchen, replete with gleaming white surfaces, implies that the cook doesn't stray beyond boiling mangetout and serving it with safe ingredients culled from one of those Sainsbury's recipe ads for the lazy and unimaginative. Serious activity in the kitchen implies wispy garlic shells falling into the cracks between the dishwasher and the cupboard, dirty walls from the smoke given off when you really do cook steak in a minute, evidence of home-made jam having boiled over when the telephone went. When in trouble, I could quote the proverb back at her.

I set about removing the manky Axminster, the estate agent's vaunted 'fitted carpets' that had come with the house. Beneath was underlay on top of hardboard, and only below that did floorboards present themselves. The hardboard came up easily enough, but at approximately two centimetre intervals it had been held down by tiny tacks which remained stubbornly in place. For their removal, no strategies presented themselves. One was to pull them all out. The other was to knock them all in. Hardboard sheets of three foot by three foot held down by tacks spaced every two centimetres equals around 140 tacks per sheet. The living room is 10ft x 24ft = 240 sq.ft., i.e. twenty-five hardboard sheets, 25 x 140 = 3,500 tacks. Take into account the hall, stairs, landing, three bedrooms, the fiddly bits around the loo = c.10,000 tacks. The nosy may pause at this point, and calculate that I have rather a small house for a stockbroker, particularly given the good value you get in downmarket Camberwell.

A time and motion study – it takes a lot of time and a lot of motion to hit a tiny tack – revealed that pulling them out takes twice as long as knocking them in, so I decided to knock them in, which takes two accurate blows of the hammer. Missing put the average up a bit, and being a Jermyn Street be-shirted executive unsullied by experience of physical travail, I missed quite a lot, so we were talking about 4 x 10,000 = 40,000 blows or so of the hammer to prepare the floor for sanding.

Rika would only be absent in whichever Riviera it was for a few days, so I had to get the job done quickly or face evisceration with a ceremonial sword annealed in a forge after the most ancient Samurai tradition, or whatever the Korean equivalent is. Rika's Dad would probably claim that Samurai traditions originated in Korea anyway. A historian of some note, he liked to say that incontrovertible evidence had been found in an archaeological dig which proved that the Emperor was Korean. The Japanese are very much into the uniqueness and purity of their race and don't like this suggestion.

The hammering took until late into the night. Accuracy was the key, but with 20,000 to hit, misses were bound to happen, either of the bend-the-nail or the whack-the-finger variety. It was not long (say 1.30 a.m.) before a be-pyjamaed Mr Gibbon arrived to complain.

A soft answer turneth away wrath, but no amount of honeyed words would placate Mr Gibbon. He was relentless, wouldn't let go – a sort of pit bull pensioner – but without his teeth in sounded like the elder Steptoe. I wasn't enjoying smiting microscopic tacks any more than he enjoyed listening to them being smitten, so the relentlessness of the verbal maiming caught me in unreceptive mood. After about ten minutes of spurned apologies I told him to bugger off. 'I'd expect a jumped-up yuppy like you to say something like that to a poor old bloke my age,' he said, as he took my advice.

In retrospect I guess that he had a point. As a pre-war member of the London Symphony Orchestra, he knew the principle whereby naked wood suspended over a body of air resonates more fully than wood clothed in carpet, underlay and hardboard. My whole house was like the inside of a violin, and was in the process of being struck 40,000 times.

The Nissan ZX substitute, the grand piano, was too big to be moved from the scene of action, so I had lovingly wrapped it in 150 metres of Safeway's own brand clingfilm, to protect its gleaming black casework, and 2,000 moving parts from the dust. A beast of promise in its very own condom. Human nature being what it is, such prophylactics occasionally fail to stand up to what is demanded of them. Gen owes his existence to one such failure.

A flash of a fingernail and I had the keyboard open. Sod it, I had been slaving all day, it was 1.30 in the morning, I was in a bad mood, Mr Gibbon had made it worse, and I needed some relaxation. I could do a passable impression of Vladimir Ashkenazy hitting the dramatic chords, struck fff in the first two bars of the 'Pathétique Sonata' (purists will point out that Beethoven suggests ff but that is considerably less fun). Thereafter, there are too many notes. About thirty minutes of 'Für Elise' later, at around 2 a.m., Mr Gibbon was back, leaning on my doorbell.

He could hear every note in every room in the house. 'Couldn't you get a job?' he hissed through his gums.

A few days later Mr Gibbon was back on my doorbell again because having knocked the tacks in, I then made an infernal din with the floor stripper. If he was a pit bull pensioner, this was a pit bull hoover, a device that drags you noisily across the floor.

He was back again a few days after that because I had to apply various poisons to the wood to inhibit the spread of woodworm, dry rot, death watch beetle, etc. The fumes, he told me, had spread through the wall and were making both the younger and the older Mrs Gibbon poorly.

He could smell every whiff in every room in the house.

The older Mrs Gibbon was blaming him because any construction work performed around this neighbourhood was generally Mr Gibbon's. Although she had the virtue, unlike her ex-husband, of being hard of hearing, she was good of smelling.

'Why don't you get yourself a bloody job?' became Mr Gibbon's refrain.

'I am trying, but in case you haven't noticed, there is a recession on,' I replied, but soon learnt to avoid such comments, which would stimulate a long discourse about the Jarrow March, and how you young people didn't know what suffering was. On reflection, probably true.

Mr Gibbon was at home with too much time on his hands for anything except moaning twenty-three and a half hours out of every twenty-four.

16

I interviewed with half a dozen more firms, and I began to get rather skilful. My skill was an academic one because none would offer me a job in my speciality.

I grew adept at fielding certain questions.

'Why were you made redundant?'

True answer: 'My chosen client base, the Japanese investor, is doing absolutely no business at the moment, and won't be for the foreseeable future, and so my company sensibly sacked me, as I was of no economic worth to them whatsoever.'

Interview answer: 'My chosen client base, the Japanese, are going through certain short-term difficulties, but it is only a matter of time before they have spondulicks like you have never seen spondulicks and will rule the world.' Not a fable I believed myself, but it was axiomatic that the Japanese were hell-bent on dominating not merely the market in Van Goghs, but every other market too. There was still a belief in the Wall of Money, but with business volumes low back in the UK, almost all companies were prepared to wait and see, i.e., not employ me.

'I see from your C.V. that you have worked for five firms in five years. Why have you worked for so many?'

The fact that three of them no longer existed was a good excuse, although it didn't augur well for my stock selection capabilities.

There is something called the Curse of Jim Parton. The first three companies I worked for in the City have all been effectively closed down. The writing may be on the wall for the fourth, UBS Phillips and Drew, which has recently changed its name to UBS Ltd. Wags are already making the obvious joke that the emphasis is on the second part of this exiting new name. Merrill Lynch should plead with me to rejoin them.

I resolved not to get caught out with this question again, and quietly removed two companies from the C.V. – they're never checked anyway.

The true answer was that I hated confronting bosses about pay, and it was much easier and more exciting, to change companies to achieve a pay rise in line with the bull market.

Occasionally an interviewer saw right through me. A Mr James Shaw was one such. 'You speak fluent Japanese, fluent French, are obviously very intelligent,' – he'd believed my skilfully insinuating C.V. on this – 'what on earth are you doing being a salesman? Soul destroying. Smile and dial. You must have some kind of plan, a strategy, to be somewhere in five years' time. What on earth have you been doing with yourself?'

I could scarcely explain to him that my languages were not that excellent, or that my brains came from Pongo Parton's side of the family. Or that I had no strategy. I had drifted into the City without the first idea of the difference between an equity and a bond. More recently, my strategy had been to pick up a couple of those famed hundred per cent bonuses (never did manage that), pay off the mortgage, then pack it all in. Plenty start off with this target, but almost all develop such financial outgoings that there is no escape. I was one such. A further burden in my case was the need to nurse a wife who had been diagnosed H.A.V. positive (Hermès Armani Vuitton; pronounce it the way it looks), a condition for which the drug companies have not yet found a cure.

I interrogated Mr Shaw in turn. He had left County Natwest during certain upheavals a few years back and gone to work in industry, which he had hated. 'Lazy, dishonest and doesn't deserve to succeed in this country,' so he had gone back into the City to help those lazy, dishonest, undeserving people raise money to run their industries.

My industrial experience was minimal. As a student, my Christmas job was on the pork pie machine at Saxby's Bros, Wellingborough. My mother is a Saxby, you see. You'd develop life enhancing skills like being able to cut exactly 10lbs of pastry off a hundred weight lump, and be only a couple of ounces out, all without using the scales. Or you'd sit next to someone on the pork pie machine, and she'd say, 'You know that Mr Saxby, he even looks like a pig...' Then I'd reply that Mr Saxby was my mother's first cousin, but don't worry, I won't say anything. As family, you'd get privileges, like doing creative stuff such as hand-crimping the top of the six-pounders destined for Harrods. An ordinary person might have had to earn his golden watch to be so trusted, yet I was allowed to crimp at just nineteen. Though not even family connections got me out of the worst job, which was squirting hot molten jelly into the pies after baking.

Thus the veracity of Mr Shaw's assertion is not one I can confirm or deny, but it is fair to say at least that City people are not lazy. Most of them are honest. As for deserving, that is a more difficult question. I had been unquestionably undeserving, even of my rather modest salary, "just a little more than the Chancellor of the Exchequer.

Another standard interview question was 'What motivates you?'

I am told that if you are being interviewed by Christopher Heath of Baring Securities, erstwhile most highly paid man in Britain, there is only one correct answer. Crap about job satisfaction, desire for responsibility, cuts no ice. You have to answer, 'Money, lots of money, then still more money, and getting rich.' This response does have the merit of being an honest one in most cases.

My ambition of paying off the mortgage, funding the education of Gen and three more putative children, then, with no debts, establishing a pleasant lifestyle in an attractive Georgian rectory in Somerset requiring only a lowish income to make it work, would, if it leaked out, be fatal to employment chances, unless I had an intelligent person interviewing me who would realise that my aim was so naïvely unrealistic that I would be working for him forever. But then he wouldn't want to employ a naïve person.

Other answers:

1.   Ambition for authority. This needs phrasing correctly. 'I want to be sitting where you are in x years time,' can sound bold, can sound threatening, usually sounds silly. It has a neat

element of flattery, if the interviewer sees himself as a bit of a role model. Most interviewers do. A thirst for authority or power would probably be a little too abstract for most hirers to consider it important. Insecure ones would also worry about the consequences of hiring someone who could be a threat to themselves.

2. The satisfaction of a job well done. You'd be laughed at for the naïve claim that doing your job well was motive enough in itself.

3. Providing a professional service to the clients. As above: idealism is not what you are paid for. In some cases, good service will produce most commission, but in others it is likely to be good Wimbledon tickets or good flattery, or some other form of human chemistry. Even unattractive blondes do well with Arab clients. There are some great gay salesmen.

4. Success and the respect (preferably envy) of one's peers. This might appeal to some narcissists, but, again, is a bit too abstract to impress, despite being the thing that drives most ambitious people.

In the City, the answer prescribed for Christopher Heath is probably the safest. Everyone knows that as broking is scarcely done for reasons of enhancing one's spirituality, money can be the only motivation.

Unless, perhaps, you can bullshit about an academic fascination with some variety of rocket science: 'I've got a computer data model which I need to develop for calculating spreads between the decay values of synthetic equity warrants, given a set of independent variables, like compounded putative interest rates over time, if the underlying equity outperforms underlying market momentum.'

Sounds good, better hire him in case it is.

Brainy academic types like this frequently get ripped off, although the smart ones do the ripping, knowing that very few people know anything at all about the insides of computers.

Blinding with science can be sustained for quite a long time; some clients like it because they in turn can blind their colleagues with it, and more importantly their funds' trustees. A trustee really feels he is getting value for money if he doesn't understand how the money in his trust is being invested. And because he doesn't understand, he never questions the huge profit margin that is mathematically built into the depths of the computer programme. Being good at maths and computers is certainly a more useful skill in the City than speaking Japanese. I know several unprepossessing train spotter/computer hacker types who earn truly dizzying sums of money.

If a fund's trustees don't understand, what price Joe Public? Unit trusts are bad for your wealth. As are most pension funds. City professionals do not buy unit trusts, knowing what proportion of the fund goes on admin, and in some cases, understanding how badly their clients invest.

The other question that is unfailingly asked is: 'What do you consider to be your greatest weakness?'

There is no choice but to lie in answer to this one. In my case an honest answer would be:

1. Bone idle.
2. Disorganised and inefficient.
3. Incapable of arriving anywhere on time.
4. Not particularly interested in the job.
5. Very forgetful – particularly names, faces, events.
6. Weak, easily manipulable character – this might just be an attractive quality to employers who are themselves weak and easily manipulable.
7. Lack of motivation – if only I could pay off my debts I would happily jack it all in. (This is important – most people who love their jobs are good at them, but it is difficult to know which is the chicken and which is the egg, being good at the job, or loving it.)

With Baring Securities's Christopher Heath, who would interview all candidates, I was advised that you should think of a nasty weakness, although I was told that 'Don't tolerate fools lightly' had been overused a little lately.

He also always asked people like me whether or not they were 'having a love affair with the Japanese (plural).' The correct answer to this is 'No', otherwise you didn't get the job. At Baring Securities, they didn't like the Japanese. I don't suppose that this has changed now that Mr Heath himself has made way for a younger man (a euphemistic description for what really happened).

I can see the eminently wise purpose of this question. It is designed to weed out all those dreamers who mistakenly believe Japan is the land of Zen, of haiku, of graceful Geisha girls, of the peaceful contemplation of moonlight, of man's harmonious interaction with nature. If I was interviewing someone, who having lived in Japan, claimed to admire these Japanese qualities, I'd worry about which planet he'd been on.

Back in London, at an interview with Baring's Mr Andrew Bayliss in 1986, I asked if they had many Japanese in their London office. 'As few as possible,' he replied.

'Why?' I asked.

'We don't like them.' Such refreshing honesty and lack of hypocrisy, from a company that has made almost all of its profits from Japanese stocks.

Barings declined to interview me this time. They remembered me from five years before, when the young walking warning that stockbroking is bad for your health, the one with the grown-up-under-a-flowerpot complexion had, insiders tell me, found me a bit too flippant.

Had I been interviewed, I think I would have claimed that my greatest weakness was arrogance, because it implies self-confidence, or perhaps impatience, as it implies a desire to get things done, and hints at dynamism. I would hope that flippancy could somehow become confused in their minds with wit, or that they might have forgotten about my regrettable trait of not taking things too seriously; in any case, the best humour is deadly serious.

When asked your strengths, there is a nice balance to be struck between being too modest and failing to get your strengths across, and claiming too much for yourself. There are weak strengths and strong strengths.

Weak strengths:

1. I like people (= wimpy liberal).
2. I am honest (= naïve).
3. I am a nice chap (= naïve wimpy liberal).
4. I work hard (everyone says that, unlikely to be believed).

Strong strengths:

1. Cast iron, provable client base and commission record that will move with you. Rare – but get two big clients to guarantee to follow you, and no broker should refuse you.
2. Instinctive, unforced clubability, i.e. good in a pub, and able to adapt to not only people from Essex and Eton, but also the lower-middle-class fund manager from Surbiton, who used to read the *Guardian*, but has now switched self-consciously to the *Telegraph*. Etonian Alick goes to the dogs with Bernie the Barrow boy from the K.I.O. (I don't think Alick is interested in the dogs), and makes the chap from Surbiton feel good about drinking Pimms at Wimbledon.
3. Intelligence. (Being streetwise better.)
4. Conscientiousness. (Difficult to prove, can imply dullness.)
5. Driving ambition or 'hunger'. This last often arises from innate insecurity. As the grandfatherly American boss at Merrill Lynch had once remarked rather profoundly, 'insecure people make the best salesmen'.

Christopher Heath asks people whether or not they are 'hungry'. He asked me this, when I met him in Japan. I said 'Yes'. It was seven-thirty in the evening, and as an English teacher down on his uppers, I fancied some freebie capitalist pig-dog scoff, so I inadvertently gave the right answer, which is why I progressed to the second interview with the flowerpot man.

Ultimately the strongest strength you can have is half a dozen mates, especially amongst the clients, who will stick up for you when they get rung up for a reference. Get those two clients with decent sized funds to stick up for you with your prospective employer, and you will always get a job. Similar rules of thumb must apply in any business in the world.

Unfortunately my best client was Mr Hoshide, who had very small funds.

17

Mr Hoshide gave me a call at home, to see how I was, and ask when he could start receiving my advice again. He invited me to dinner.

As the local, I selected a Chinese restaurant in Soho, and we had a very pleasant meal. Mr Hoshide commiserated with me about not having been able to give me more business, he said that he almost blamed himself for my redundancy. The Gulf War and the Tokyo stock market collapse had lead to a panicky head office, and left him with permission to do maintenance dealing only, so that there had been very little business for me.

'We Japanese have small...' he paused on a mouthful of noodles, '...funds.'

I liked Mr Hoshide, he'd been a good, loyal client, but I knew that he operated under more constraints than he could let on. Size wasn't the only one.

Another was the necessity to give a large portion of his business to his Japanese brokers, and so although the likes of Nomura had little in the way of proprietary information to offer about Europe, they almost certainly had been getting the lion's share of the business. Nigel, newly ensconced at Nomura Securities, had told me the mouth-watering commission figures of my direct competitor there, a Japanese with less than a couple of years of experience of the European markets.

Mr Hoshide worked for a very large insurance company indeed. This meant that when things went wrong with its investments, his company was amongst the first to be compensated by Nomura, by juggling investments around, usually at the expense of Japan's typical small investor, Mrs Watanabe, the bored housewife from Niigata Prefecture, who, throughout the 1980s, was gambling the family finances on stocks and shares, in between visits to the local Louis Vuitton outlet.

Nomura, Daiwa, Nikko and Yamaichi were eventually forced to apologise to the world for compensating important clients at the expense of less important ones. A book called *The House of Nomura* by Al Alletzhauser alleged that Nomura had connections with gangsters, and also compensated certain clients. Nomura denied this and sued for libel. Even as Nomura was admitting the allegations in Japan, its lawyers in London were still threatening to take Mr Alletzhauser all the way to trial. It's a pity they didn't. All sorts of dirty linen would have been washed, and the Western public might have begun to understand that Japan is as corrupt, if not more so, than Italy, or any of the ex-communist countries, or most of Africa. Sensibly, though, Nomura backed off, and didn't get nearly as much egg on their faces as they deserved.

Westerners commonly feel sorry for the downtrodden Mrs Watanabe of Niigata Prefecture, bound as she is to the home and banned from having a career. This sympathy is mistaken because she has infinitely more power and freedom than her poor husband, who, when he isn't stuck at the office, has to spend insufferable, drunken karaoke evenings out with his colleagues. Mr Hoshide, for example, candidly admitted to me that because he gets pissed in zero seconds flat, and his doctor has said that this is bad for him, he has to mime his frivolity. He is quite droll when drunk, going bright-red in the face, and saying in English, which he must have got straight from a P.G. Wodehouse book, 'Forgive me, it's my enzymes playing up.'

I know this to be true. I used to teach English conversation to a group of three consultant urologists at Osaka University Hospital, one of the top medical establishments in the country. My students told me that the Japanese as a race do not have enough of a crucial enzyme involved in the breakdown of alcohol, which is why they get drunk very quickly.

Poor Mr Hoshide miming his frivolity. This is a hell of a burden. I mean, how many people in Britain, say, hand on heart, really enjoy the company of the people they work with? Would choose them as friends? Do we invite our colleagues to dinner out of anything more than a sense of duty? Or a desire to enhance career prospects?

What, one asks, was my motive in inviting Alick skiing? Love of Alick?

A lot is made of the drinking custom to explain Japan's harmonious industrial relations. While drunk, a man can air his dissatisfaction, and criticise his boss with impunity. If drunk, the boss, subliminally at least, takes the criticism on board and reacts to it, but does not hold it against the subordinate. This is of course untrue. If Mr Hoshide, while pissed, were to say too many harsh things about his boss, he would be plucked from the heady world of international investment banking in London, his next posting to be selling life assurance policies door-to-door in Fukuoka.

The Japanese woman is spared all this. She is more or less barred from meeting her husband's colleagues, the lucky thing. In addition, by custom, he hands over his entire wage packet at the end of the month, usually in cash, and is then given pocket money for going out on karaoke nights. She is free to spend the rest on the home, education for the 1.3 children (low birth rate in Japan), and blow what remains after that on Hermès scarves, Armani suits, and Vuitton bags, and once the child is in school, on tennis or ikebana lessons, coffee mornings with the girls or other diversions. (Another diversion is an affair with her English teacher - sadly I missed out on this aspect of Japanese culture.) Door-to-door salesmen do good trade with her, and include stockbrokers, and Mr Hoshide's life assurance salesmen. In households where the money has gone, the Mormons and Jehovah's Witnesses do reasonably well too.

The archetypal Mrs Watanabe of Niigata Prefecture was strangely stoical about being stuffed in at the top of most market moves, presumably because she was too unsophisticated to notice that she was being done. When the movements of Japan's markets were inexorably upwards, the fact that her investments were going up less than the average was something she didn't notice. Now that markets were moving inexorably in the down direction, her losses were beginning to look rather stark. She was starting to ask questions about the wisdom of following the advice of her local Nomura salesman. The losses she was incurring were threatening her consumption of Louis Vuitton bags. I imagine her English teacher has become a bit too expensive to run too.

With sources of commission income such as Mrs Watanabe beginning to dry up, Nomura were calling in a few favours, and I could well guess that poor Mr Hoshide couldn't give me as much business as he'd have liked.

Wronged clients of the big four securities houses have started to make a bit of a fuss, and Nomura, Daiwa, Nikko and Yamaichi have all at some stage or other had to make public apologies and pay fines or compensation for misdemeanours which in Britain or America might close them down.

It is likely that so far revealed are the tips of icebergs of corruption. Indeed we have probably only got as far as the snowball on the tip of the iceberg. Robert Maxwell may well come to seem quite a nice man in comparison to some of the people in big Japanese securities houses. The sums of money so far revealed in scandals already dwarf the minor fiasco that was BCCI.

Certain British fund managers must be hoping that not too much comes out. I know of one fund manager at a very blue-chip UK insurance company who received a Ferrari in return for directing his business through one of the Big Four. He was found out, and quietly, very quietly, sacked.

In Tokyo, a certain amount of handing over of anonymous-looking brown envelopes goes on. For a Western fund manager in Tokyo, receiving a bribe is pretty much risk free. If his company finds out, it is scarcely likely to sack him publicly. They are much more likely to hush it up. The Japanese authorities would be being spectacularly hypocritical if they were to prosecute. The fund manager is at a safe distance from the investment watchdogs in the UK or the US.

Until recently, in Tokyo, Western fund managers who did a trade in the morning could, and did, book it to their own private stock account in the afternoon if it had gone up, to their client's fund if not. Japanese brokers co-operated with this, and ended up picking up a lot of business as a result. My understanding is that such corruption was not limited to the Japanese, but that British and American brokers did the same. It is, after all, a practice that was commonplace in the City, until regulators started to have power.

The Japanese Ministry of Finance is supposed to keep things in check, but it is impossible to imagine that its members are not kept sweet in the same way as fund managers. Occasionally the MoF does a raid on brokers, but nearly always warns of its arrival in advance. Unless the broker is foreign, of course.

Raids on foreign brokers are likely to have less to do with corruption than the fact that foreign brokers have been doing more business in Tokyo than Japanese ones of late. This is because the big American and British brokers are way ahead in futures and options and other instruments where the profit margin is buried safely out of sight in the depths of the computer programme, in a way that few clients understand. And even fewer people from the MoF.

Mr Hoshide was just a foot soldier in the middle of all these events, and so was I. He quietly got on with his job of supplying information to Tokyo about our European markets, and I would supply him with arcane stuff about the UK investment trust industry, or the result of the official West German distributive trades survey, and its implications for the West German economy, and race riots in Brandenburg.

Nice chap, Mr Hoshide. He paid for the meal, a reversal of roles which I quite enjoyed, and expressed solidarity with me in my time of trouble. A talented stockbroker I was not, but then neither were all my problems entirely to be laid at my door. I shook hands with him outside the restaurant, and directed him towards a taxi. His enzymes had let him down again, and he was a bit drunk, in a benign sort of way. 'I am sorry, Mr Parton, about my size,' he kept on muttering.

I caught the stares of a few passers-by, and wanted to say to them, this man does not mean what you think he means.

18

I had been out of work for two months. The job hunt, it must be said, wasn't going particularly well. No one had got close to offering me a job, although I had had the odd second interview.

Rory's Dad drew a blank suing Merrill Lynch over my dismissal. Had I not signed that crucial document agreeing to severance terms that the likes of Nigel had advised me were reasonable, I might have squeezed more out of them, if only because the opposition prefer to avoid untoward hassle, and a few thousand here or there makes no difference to them.

The obvious lesson is that if you are made redundant, check with a clued-up solicitor before you sign anything. Quite a few people of my acquaintance have successfully agitated to keep the company car, for example.

The garden was looking better and better, the train set had acquired a few mountains and I had sorted out the vagaries of the electrics. Hostilities between myself and Mr Gibbon had reached a state of uneasy truce, but truce nonetheless.

I compared happy holidays in France with the grey misery of London. Perhaps London was not the place for me, but Tokyo looked difficult: employing Gaijins was too expensive. The tendency was to send them back and replace them with local Japanese. Various friends of mine are back in Britain now as reverse tax exiles. After five years in Tokyo you start to pay Japanese taxes at the full rate, so the trend for overpaid brokers is to come back and do a year in London, with the aim of starting out again tax free in Tokyo. (Your first few years are tax free – it gradually increases until you pay full whack: ethnic cleansing, Japanese style.) In practice, once back in London, many find the competition for clients too stiff, and end up on the scrap heap like me. Their descent is brutally abrupt, from earning, say, £250,000 tax free, to zero. If they decide that Tokyo was the place after all, they discover that their job has not waited for them. The years of mad bonanza are over.

I tried Madrid and Milan by telephone, but in both places, whilst encountering enthusiasm, ran up against the siesta effect. They were all too disorganised to do anything. Paris on the other hand was a different matter. Broking is more developed there than in other European cities, and you can pop across for the day for an interview.

The light at the end of the Chunnel was Verona, whose friend Xavier was over in London with his French bosses. I was soon shaking hands with Didier Fauchier Magnan and Monsieur Antoine Durant des Aulnois whose names I supply with the benefit of hindsight, because at the time I didn't quite catch them. When we parted, their postcard-sized business cards read 'Société de Bourse Fauchier Magnan Durant des Aulnois'. Silly me for not having heard of them.

I wondered where Monsieur Durant des Aulnois got all the bits to his surname. There had been something distinctly nouveau about him. His real name was probably Jean Dupont.

Fauchier Magnan appeared to accept my argument that now that everyone was cutting back their business to the Japanese, it was a good time to be setting one up. Privately, I thought that this theory was probably wrong. Going against the economic cycle can be very clever; if you had sold your house in 1988 as everyone else was in a buying frenzy you would be feeling pretty damn smug by now. But had you done the opposite to everybody else two years earlier, you would be looking pretty damn stupid.

Messieurs Fauchier Magnan and Durant des Aulnois ran the risk of looking pretty damn stupid if they employed me.

Xavier confided afterwards that the two multi-barrelled Frenchmen had been quite impressed by me. He thought that the interview had gone quite well.

'Are you coming to Paris sometime?' I was asked.

Not so damn stupid. Partnerships care about costs, and if they could get away without funding my flight to Charles de Gaulle they would. Better to work for a brokerage owned by a bank; banks don't understand brokers, but for some reason like owning them. Costs accordingly spiral, amongst them salesmen's pay.

Donald the headhunter rang. 'Hi, Jim, how's tricks?' He sounded over the moon to speak to me again. He told me to ring Graham Butcher at the aptly named Société de Bourse Oddo, who were interested in me. On the phone, Graham explained how he'd been out of work for three months. 'By the end of that my balls were burning. I was constantly told I was too old – at thirty-seven – too senior, I wouldn't fit in with younger people in a junior position. I wouldn't be satisfied, they all said. To me it wasn't a question of satisfaction, but one of survival.'

'Are you coming to Paris sometime?' I wondered which of the interviewing companies I would get to pay for the flight, or whether perhaps I could get them all to pay. This would be a cinch for any decent broker.

Verona's chum Xavier agreed to have me to stay.

Coming in from the airport I had been struck by how clean and efficient the trains were and in the Metro, how much better the buskers. No desultory Dylan dirgers here. Leaving London would be no wrench.

Xavier's flat was on the sixth floor of a building, a broker's garret, not quite a penthouse. About twenty-six, and, despite the name, English, he was five years younger than Verona, good-looking and doing well. He was clearly loving Paris. It struck me that Verona's Trans Manche Link, a combination of young bachelor in Paris, and professional girl in her early thirties beginning to worry about the ticking of the biological clock, was doomed.

In the evening we went to a party of young expatriate Brits with a token French person or two, and plenty of vying to affect the best French accents. Everybody seemed to love Paris, and I decided, as if I needed persuading, that I wanted to live there too, away from London and its filthy streets, inefficient tubes and over-taxed booze.

I was all for staying until the small hours but Xavier had to get up early for work, so we left the party early. My attitude to such things had changed starkly. Getting out in the evening to escape my own company was becoming the most important part of the day for me, whereas previously it had been getting home, and into bed by ten or so, in order not to be knackered the next day.

* * *

I got up at 10.45 for an 11.30 interview followed by lunch chez Oddo. I needed some good strong coffee to get me going but remembered to resist temptation. My weak bladder and high metabolic rate had stood me in good stead when negotiating with Merrill Lynch, but I couldn't count on it a second time. Coffee gives me a brief buzz before racing for freedom. Combined with interview nerves it could be quite disruptive. I also remembered not to drink water for the same reason. I badly needed some because my head hurt from the night before, but I knew there were sufficient unmetabolised poisons in my bloodstream for several trips *au pissoir*. It was best that they remained unmetabolised. When one is holding one's own in a discussion of French fiscal policy with the senior partner of a broking firm, one doesn't want to be holding one's own, or even folding one's own.

The interview with Monsieur Oddo went quite well. Graham was on my side because he knew me from Scrimgeour Vickers days, but not well enough to know how little business I did. He might have twigged because when he introduced me to one of the Oddo dealers, an Englishman also from Scrimgeours, we didn't recognise each other.

Graham told me he used to fancy my sister and was at Oxford with my brother, so I began to consider the job virtually mine.

In France I would be able to restart the whole cycle of selling myself, followed by selling the idea of my client base to the French (*le mur d'argent arrive*), right down to the point where it was discovered that *le mur d'argent n'arrivera plus*.

Monsieur Oddo was a nice enough fellow, who had just inherited his firm. He was about my age.

'*Combien est-ce que vous gagniez.*'

'*Soixante-cinq mille livres.*'

'*Vous pouvez baisser un peu?*'

Was I to have female clients only, I found myself wondering before getting his drift. As a partner in the family firm, he had a real interest in paying as little as possible.

I dodged the issue of pay by saying that I had no idea what people got paid in Paris or about the cost of living. Pay was the only serious question he asked me, there was nothing on my weaknesses or why I was made redundant. It is strange how such people focus on what you should be paid, but rarely, if ever, ask what they would get for their money.

This 'interview' was followed by a very pleasant lunch with Graham. He talked a lot, so although exposed to the possibility of saying something silly for over an hour and a half, I was rarely given the chance to do so.

Graham, like Xavier, loved Paris. The cost of living was very similar to London, it was swings and roundabouts. 'Cars, smoking, drinking, eating out and sex are cheaper, groceries, clothes, petrol, and housing are more expensive.'

I was not quite sure what he meant when he said that sex was cheaper. Was he referring to the ladies in the Bois de Boulogne, or did he mean the whole process of dinner and a show followed by viewing of etchings? Or perhaps he felt that French women are desperate because so many French men are pooftahs, although I had always been told by the French that they regarded English men as being somewhat effeminate, which is why suave Frogs can be such fearsome predators in Britain.

Despite, or perhaps because of, my marriage to someone from a different race and culture, I hold highly offensive, and politically incorrect views about such relationships. But empirical observations made over a period of years make me sure that I am right.

Namely, there must be something wrong with French men, from the point of view of French women. In Japan, it is quite rare for Western women to marry Japanese men, but it always struck me that there was an unusually high number of French women who did this. For other nationalities, the pattern is the reverse; white men marry yellow women, as I did, and very rarely the other way round, rather as in Britain you see numerous black men with white women, but much less commonly the reverse.

It all boils down to sex; from the point of view of a Western man in Japan, small is cute, large is not, and so white women wander the streets of Japan, remaining sexually frustrated because they find teeny-weeny Japanese men unattractive, and the Western men are only interested in Japanese women. 'It gives you a whole new slant on life,' as one broker friend explained to me.

There are only a couple of categories which are exceptions to this rule. One is hugely fat American women, who are popular with Japanese men on account, one speculates, of a fascination with the vastness of their mammaries. These are not a novelty to fellow Americans. Loneliness, and gratitude, at finding a man happy to be smothered, undoubtedly play their part in leading many of these couples into marriage, as well as the excitement of being in a mixed culture marriage, an excitement that can appeal to all categories of people everywhere.

The other category is French women. In Japan, I observed a lot of Françoise Yamamotos. I could only theorise that they found Japanese men reassuringly familiar, with their obsessiveness about sex, and their treatment of women like shit.

Another characteristic that the French share with the Japanese is a certain slavish conformity, a need to be safely regulated in society. In Japan, you will see groups on corporate outings all wearing identical anoraks. In Britain almost never, but in France often. Wander the streets of Paris and by the time you have worked out the subtle differences between each social grouping, you will see that the French wear what are effectively uniforms.

Personally I pay little attention to the way I dress – it just doesn't interest me – and am happiest in a favourite sweater riddled with holes and trousers which won't show the dirt if you wipe your hands on them when you are gardening or cooking. A French girlfriend of my youth would always accuse me of wearing scruffy clothes on purpose, with the aim of drawing attention to myself. She couldn't bring herself to believe my protestations that my style of dressing was entirely unaffected, foreshadowing 'grunge' by a good fifteen years.

All this is not quite a digression; I was in Paris to get a job, and one thing for consideration was, would I fit in? Rika would, at least. It is not just that the French are innately conformist, and thus have things in common with the Japanese, they are also admirers of the Japanese culturally. It may have started with the Impressionists who were Impressed by Ukiyo-e wood block prints often carelessly used as wrapping paper round imported ceramics in the later nineteenth century. It continues with Japanese fashion designers doing far better in Paris than in London, and the films of Kurosawa doing far better there than in London, or even Tokyo. A romantic lot the French, because they have an ideal of Japan that no longer exists. Modern Japanese culture is schmaltz, chintz, kitsch, Japsch.

Paris seemed like a good idea for me too. It would be fun. Gen would end up tri-lingual. The Alps would be a viable weekend away. The only big question would be whether or not I would be sufficiently conformist to fit in. I'd have a certain advantage as a foreigner; by pretending not to know the ground rules you can get away with a lot, just as I used to in Japan. I used to feel that it was a positive duty, for example, to walk across the road when the pedestrian light was red, but there were no cars coming. Until one day I did it in front of a wizened little old lady, age approximately eighty-five, bent double from a lifetime sitting cross-legged and reaching down to plant rice seedlings in paddy fields. She did a double take at my audacity, paused, then almost stepped into the path of an oncoming car, before retreating back behind the line where you are supposed to wait when the light is still red, which it was. She didn't say anything, but there was a look of hurt and confusion in her eyes, like a rabbit which has just been shot, is not quite dead, and is trying to work out what went wrong.

I felt as though I had mugged her, and disgusted at myself, never jaywalked again in Japan.

Cutting loose and breaking free is very difficult. In the City I had flirted with checked shirts. It is quite common on Friday afternoons for upper-middle-class bimbos to come round broking offices selling (on commission) brogues and stripy double cuffed shirts. After a good lunch you are vulnerable, and also, given that these girls are always the sister of somebody in the dealing room's best friend, peer pressure does the rest. They do a very healthy trade indeed.

Having bought a checked shirt with double cuffs, I mentioned to a colleague at Phillips and Drew that I would wear it to the office. He said that if I did he would never speak to me again. He wasn't someone that I admired, so this threat should have been no sanction, but even so, he was voicing what everyone else thought, so I never did wear my checked shirt with double cuffs to the office. What a pathetic coward.

I suppose that my theory that the Japanese and French are slavishly conformist, and that the British, starting with me, aren't, has its shortcomings. Go into a media pub in Soho, and lined up on bar stools will be five men with ponytails. You wonder whether, if you pull one of them, beer will come out. A ponytail looks like a bit of a statement, a bit of anti-Establishment bravado, but is in fact just another uniform.

The only time nonconformity is acceptable at work is if you are brilliant at your job. Nobody says to John Harvey-Jones that he looks a mess and needs a haircut, whereas people used to say it to me all the time.

Still, if I got a job in Paris I could play the bluff, slightly eccentric Englishman at the same time as promising great things from my client base. '*Il est fou, il est anglais, mais le mur d'argent arrive.*'

I was careful neither to drink nor eat too much as I still had a couple of meetings arranged for later in the afternoon, and after a big meal, sleep was the enemy. I said goodbye to Graham and wended my way.

Fauchier Magnan Durant des Aulnois was quite difficult to find, as had been Oddo. Both companies were behind discreet doors with just a number on them, on the principle, I suppose, that the best brothels don't advertise. Neither looked as a stockbrokers should; there was no glass atrium covering five floors, no ostentatious logo on a brass plaque set in Carrera (I misspell it like the eponymous Porsche) marble. Broking is not a high status occupation in France. The third sons of the aristocracy in Britain might, having eschewed the Church and the Army, become 'something in the City', but in France – indeed as in the rest of Europe and Japan – broking is a low status profession. Brokers are tolerated for their money, but essentially looked down upon.

Having identified the right door and walked up to a reception area without a receptionist, I found that the company was ill prepared to interview me. It was a Friday and the various Brits had either gone for the weekend or were still at lunch, a tradition lost to the City with Big Bang in 1986, and the arrival of all those lean hungry American banks (and the fat hungry Swiss ones). The fact that the weekend still started at about midday on Friday in France, was another good, if not pivotal, reason for working there.

French broking partnerships are gradually going the way of British ones in selling out to the banks. Broking used to be very civilised; into work by half past nine, a long leisurely lunch, leave for home at half past four. In good years the rewards were spectacular, in bad ones the partners dug deep into their pockets, mortgaged their houses and kept the firm afloat. With banks in charge, pay is always spectacular but bears only a slender relationship with profitability.

French broking had already moved towards British, in that days started too early in the morning and went on too late, a collective mania for staying on at work unnecessarily, but at least Friday lunchtime was intact. I doubt very much that the extra hours lead to extra business being done, it is just another example of 'Extraordinary Popular Delusions and the Madness of Crowds', the title of a book by Charles Mackay, surprisingly approachable given that it was written in 1841. It describes the South Sea Bubble,

Tulipomania and other booms and busts, as well as collective follies, such as believing in alchemy or that witches (a) exist and (b) should be burnt. A must read, even if you only want to understand why so many people go berserk then faint at Spice Girls' concerts. People lost fortunes in tulips in seventeenth century Holland, and the price has never recovered. You can still buy a dozen bulbs for £2.50 at Homebase. I wonder when people will realise that gold, while pretty, is more or less completely useless. I guess that mania is more than 4,000 years old and may endure. Anyway, everyone should read this book.

Eventually somebody arrived, we had a brief chat, I shook hands with one or two people whose names and significance I instantly forgot, said hi to Xavier, exchanged greetings with Monsieur Durant des Aulnois and Monsieur Fauchier Magnan and that was that. It scarcely merited the accolade 'interview'.

At about four, I squeezed in one more meeting with J.P. Morgan's subsidiary. This was more like it. I travelled up seven floors of glass atrium in a restored Art Deco lift, just off the Place de l'Opera. I was kept waiting about thirty minutes. It was now 4.30 in the afternoon, Friday, Paris, and they were still working. This was not the firm for me.

A sharp-suited Frenchman of the kind with degrees from both the Harvard Business School and INSEAD grilled me for quarter of an hour before visibly losing interest, and I was back on the street before five.

Never mind. The trip to Paris certainly appeared as though it might net me two jobs, and J.P. Morgan had looked far too much like the broking subsidiary of an American bank.

Back at Heathrow it was the usual story. Sunny in Paris, cloudy over the Channel, which looks lovely from an aeroplane, raining at Heathrow, horrible from all angles. My mind was made up; Paris it would be.

19

Money was still holding out although I was having to be a little careful. Rika didn't seem to be terribly bothered by considerations of economy and conspicuous consumption remained the order of the day. Returning from her latest trip she was equipped with a new purchase of Charles Jourdan shoes. She was earning, and I could hardly criticise. I was the one without a job.

I reckoned that I could visit the dole office without losing too much self-esteem.

Alick had once remarked that he would never claim the dole, it would affront his dignity. My moral backbone was less stiff. I didn't exactly need the money, but what is National Insurance if it doesn't actually mean insurance? Besides, the forty quid a week would be a handy adjunct to my play money, and maybe I could get the mortgage paid.

The Peckham DSS is a piece of 1970s council architecture surrounded by vandalised buildings. It is in a nicely laid out courtyard, but the flowerbeds are filled with weeds, and the saplings planted in the late Seventies clearly died in the early Eighties.

A sign directed me to go up the stairs to where one is interviewed for the dole. A callow youth with a curtain ring through his nose made it plain that I was not to be allowed upstairs until he had barged me back down again with his mountain bike.

It looked rather a nice mountain bike, and I could see why he had taken it upstairs with him rather than chain it to the saplings outside.

I joined a queue resembling a United Nations High Commission for Refugees poster. Richard Claydermann-like Muzak tinkled softly overhead and I was unsure which was uglier, the music or a white woman with a shaved head and nose ring. There was the odd older white man, with the resigned look of someone who has been through it all before: London docker 1960s, car production line worker 1970s, GLC cleaner 1980s. As a young man I was near the beginning of the cycle: stockbroker 1990s.

I was interviewed by a Ghanaian lady, who asked me accusingly why it had taken two whole months to start making my claim, and warned that it was unlikely to be backdated. She asked if I had been doing any part-time jobs. There was paint on my fingernails from colouring in the mountains on the train set, so she probably thought I had been moonlighting. I was feeling generous so I didn't really mind. In any case, she ought to have been able to tell that I was in a slightly different category from her usual customer. I might not have shaved for five days but that was because I was an idle sod and not because I wanted to blend in with the surroundings.

The bald girl must spend a considerable time shaving her head each morning before going out. You slightly wonder why she didn't bother with her armpits.

I was given forms to take home and fill in to claim community charge relief, housing relief and income support. The deal sounded better and better.

Back home there turned out to be a little more small print than I had at first envisaged. My savings were still too great for me to qualify. If I paid off a chunk of the mortgage to reduce the savings it would leave me with no money to pay the mortgage. Tricky.

A few days later several letters dropped through the letter box. One was from the company car man, demanding payment of that outstanding parking fine.

20th June 1991

Dear Mr Parton,

We are still waiting for payment of £32 outstanding on your parking fine incurred on 19th December 1990. Please send payment by return. We would warn you that unless you pay you will become liable for bailiffs costs (£90).

Yours sincerely,

The nasty company car man at Merrill Lynch

I binned it immediately.

There were also two letters from Paris. Both jobs had fallen through. At Fauchier they were unwilling to have their earnings diluted for the sake of the long term.

At Oddo they were just too disorganised to make a decision. A few weeks later I got a phone call from Graham Butcher announcing that he had been laid off again, and was back on the streets.

20

I answered an ad in *The Times*: 'Career at a Crossroads? We will find the right job for you whether you are redundant or merely seeking a change. No obligation – first consultation free.' i.e. all subsequent consultations very expensive. I arrived at the door of a smart West End address. I was taken in to see a Mr Philip Tenison, fifty-five-ish, cavernous eyes, domed head, well spoken, smooth. We started with a discussion of my life so far. They had already ascertained what I had been earning from my telephone call. I am always surprised how easy it is to get such private information from me.

He glanced through my C.V. to establish my pedigree. 'Of course we will produce a more professional C.V. for you.' He wheedled out of me how much redundancy money I had been paid, thereby sussing out what the market, i.e. me, could bear in the way of fees.

'We only take on clients where we are sure that there is a future – it is a waste of our time and their money to take on no-hopers,' he said sanctimoniously. The fact that this business was booming, with guilty employers paying out-placement agencies to 'counsel out' staff they were trimming, presumably helped them be so selective. 'In your case James, I emphatically believe that you are exactly the kind of person we can help fulfil his potential.' Flattery – a standard sales technique. I often used it myself. I wondered why a well-spoken man of fifty-five like himself was doing a sales job like this. Presumably his own career had been at a crossroads in the not too distant past.

He expounded on the Tenison method. He had all the answers, without really saying anything. It was a bit like talking to the Delphic Oracle.

'What you need James, I can tell, is a charismatic leader.'

My God, how true, I thought, how did he work that out? Answer: there isn't a person in the world who wouldn't benefit from a charismatic leader. It's like saying that 'On Thursday the moon will be in conjunction with Mars and you will experience an event to disrupt your domestic tranquillity.' Well quite, I have an argument with my wife virtually every day.

A lot of what he said did make good sense.

Only twenty per cent of jobs are advertised and of those, many are only advertised because they have to be because of company rules or statutes; somebody internally or externally has already been lined up for the job vacancy, which is the case for a large proportion of the remainder of jobs too.

His promise was to help me target the unadvertised jobs market. He would also help me develop my networking skills.

Networking skills? What are they? You ring up acquaintances, even distant ones, and ask their advice. You don't say 'I'm redundant can you help get me a job,' which may not even incite sympathy because you become an instant burden to the person you are talking to. Or if they were sympathetic, it would be the wrong kind of sympathy, the kind I imagine that you would get if you were to tell someone you were terminally ill. That person could scarcely be anything other than sympathetic, but equally, would be unsure how to react, and completely unable to look you in the eye.

On the other hand, people are flattered to be asked for advice, and although the acquaintance himself may not be able to help, he may know someone who can, so you string him along until he introduces you to someone a bit nearer your Target Area (definitely said with capital letters), explained Mr Tenison. By the time you are on to the third person in the chain, you are probably down to someone in your T.A. able to interview you for a job. If you are introduced, even as a friend of a friend of a friend, it is much more likely that you will be seen, even if it is only to give you some kindly advice as to where it would be better to look.

A further advantage is that you have bypassed the personnel department. I had always thought it important to miss out personnel departments in the City, but Mr Tenison explained that this was just as important outside the City. They have the job of filtering people out rather than in. Filling in the application form, he said, is delayed as long as possible, preferably until the job is already in the bag. These are negative documents designed to weed you out, not weed you in.

Mr Tenison was talking my language. Personnel people are not at the coalface, doing a proper job. Good ones (from their own point of view) create bureaucracies round themselves. They pen urgent memos about corporate pension plans. The manager who thought that farming out recruitment to personnel would save work soon discovers that he spends just as much time filling in forms and answering memos; if he is not concentrating he will be taken in and get the impression that the personnel department is doing really good work, and thank his lucky stars that he has one to save him so much labour. The skilful personnel director will tread a fine line between overloading managers at the coalface, and creating work for them to demonstrate how indispensable he (or more likely she) is.

We had been talking for forty-five minutes. This level of service, in this level of premises, from a professional man only a little short of twice my age did not come cheaply, that was for sure. I wondered how many sales he needed to make a week to justify his existence, and what his cut was. He would have to be working on commission, not salary; I could tell that from the intensity of the spiel.

I was not being pressurised to make up my mind there and then, however. Indeed, Mr Tenison assured me that he didn't believe in the hard sell; 'That would be most unprofessional.' Now was not the time to make a decision, he told me. I was to sleep on it and above all I must consult my wife, and explain to her how the Tenison Method (more capital letters) would work for me. Nagging wives were obviously an important part of the commercial equation. He must pick up a lot of business from men pressurised into 'doing something' by wives fed up with having them moping around the home.

If Mr Tenison had known about Mr Gibbon, he would no doubt have tried to get him in on the act, too.

Rika – he'd picked up the name from somewhere, and, consummate professional that he was, was pronouncing it correctly – and I were also to discuss what breed of dog we felt I most resembled as an aid to the analysis of my character. Mr Tenison said that he would do the same, and that almost invariably he would come up with the same one.

The next day a bit more was explained. The first ten days would be spent with a psychologist and a counsellor who between them would work out my strengths and failings and come up with my Key Unique Abilities, My Ambitions, My Opportunities, otherwise known by the somewhat unwieldy acronym, as my K.U.A.M.A.M.O. list. This sounded to me more like a Central African guerilla organisation than the key to a successful career, but I was prepared to listen.

A jolly little flow diagram was produced with arrows leading to various boxes centring on 'YOU'. This would yield information, which we would use to Target (this word was used rather a lot) certain areas of human endeavour that suited me. We would conduct an Examination of Total Job Market and then devise a Marketing Campaign. It sounded splendid. We would use my networks and we would also be aware of which newspapers carry what job adverts on what days.

He had started saying 'we' rather than 'you'.

Ultimately we were going to find my Ideal Job, and negotiate a high salary; once the Target Company had recognised my Key Unique Abilities it would not want to lose me, and would cough up to retain me. Wunderbar!

What dog had I decided I most resembled? I had clean forgotten to give this any consideration at all. I was also supposed to have asked Rika. If I had ever got her to answer she might have described me as something like the offspring of an Old English Sheepdog and a passing stray which nobody saw, brought up on a very muddy farm.

If I were to do the same exercise in reverse, because Pekinese or Chow would have most unfair racial overtones, I would say something like King Charles Spaniel.

Was the congress of two such disparate animals likely to be a success? You have to feel sorry for the spaniel, but might be quite envious of the farm dog of uncertain provenance.

Mr Tenison had decided that I was like an Afghan. Sleek, smooth, physically energetic.

Surely some mistake.

Unless he was trying to tell me that if I wanted to get a job I had let my standards slip a bit and should get a haircut first. I wondered if he ever described potential clients as Pit bull, Chihuahua, Poodle, Rhodesian Ridgeback or Yorkshire Terrier. Physically energetic maybe; sleek, smooth never. Flattery – standard sales technique.

The meeting was winding down. It had all been terribly upbeat. I would achieve my Long-Term Objectives. I would love my job, operate at my Full Potential, be stretched and challenged, be recognised as a High Achiever by colleagues, be self-motivated, Implement or Affect company policy, be proud of my organisation, be surrounded by intellectually stimulating people, socially and culturally (which would make a change from the City), and best of all my wife would adore me because I would come home so satisfied that I would be in a permanently good mood and become a wonderful husband. My satisfaction would enable me to satisfy her.

Phew. What could this job be, personal sex therapist to Madonna? When could I start?

How could I use my network to get this job? I have a cousin who is the tennis correspondent on the *Daily Mail*, he'd have a mate on the pop pages, who'd have a chum in New York intimate with Madonna. All I had to do then was to prove myself the possessor of an organ of inexhaustible tumescence and I'd be away. (On second thoughts, I think Madonna is hugely overrated.)

Mr Tenison leant back in his chair, the orbs in his sockets widened, hands were rubbed together. He then leant forward again, a column of ash was knocked off his Panatella. We were getting down to the nitty-gritty. There was no disguising the fact that this one would cost £5,500, in instalments, with no money back guarantee if you failed to get a job.

'We don't offer a guarantee; if you are prepared to pay, it means you are serious, and you are much more likely to be committed. As I said before, we don't deal with no-hopers,' he said, making it sound as if not offering a guarantee was for my own good. 'But remember, there is no need to make up your mind now. We do no hard sell here, that would be most unprofessional.'

Doing no hard sell must be tough; the fundamental rule of salesmanship is that having created the desire, you have to close the sale. Perhaps he had spotted that the desire was something with which I was not exactly salivating. Or perhaps professional products like these have to be left with the client for a bit.

'I want you to go home and discuss this with Rika,' he said, giving me the sheaf of glossy papers with 'K.U.A.M.A.M.O.' and 'YOU' on it, dotted with expressions like Full Potential, High Achiever, and Personal Life Goal Attainment.

'The question is not "Can you afford it?" it is "Can you afford not to do it?" You have some redundancy money, do you have any savings?'

I was buggered if I was going to admit to any so I said 'No'.

'Would Merrill Lynch pay for it?' I think that the abortive attempt at suing them had put paid to that one.

'We can also help you with a government, interest-free loan. They ask you to chip in something yourself, but will pick up the rest. We usually find that our costs are comfortably covered by the extra salary we help you to negotiate and also we find that our clients get back to work much quicker than people who don't use us, often by several months.' This was quite a compelling sales line. He was making out that although the service cost £5,500, it was free really.

Mr Tenison wouldn't quite allow his Marty Feldmann-like orbs to meet mine as we shook hands on parting. I thought that he suspected he'd lost his man, which as I disappeared down the street I reflected that he probably had. £5,500! With all my spare time, if I couldn't supply £5,500 worth of job hunting effort myself, I was a hopeless case, besides which he had pretty much told me how to do it.

Rika was of the same opinion. 'Don't waste your money, Jim,' and was kind enough to add, 'because you haven't got any'.

I would have been slightly happier if she had said 'we', like Mr Tenison.

21

The sun was shining, and the weather in the month of May was promising a good summer. It was the time of year when cricket starts to come back on the wireless. The train set was absorbing and growing. Gen and Rory, a bit of a handful when together, were still delightful in their way. I picked up a brace of long-range water pistols for them from the car boot sale, to encourage in them a healthy interest in boyish things like guns, and subvert completely Rory's Mum's ineffectual attempts to introduce political correctness.

Cowboys are good, Red Indians are bad. Life's certainties have gone out of the window. Now it is good cowboys are good, and bad cowboys are bad. Native Americans are out of a job.

I taught them how to choose which of them was to be the baddy. 'Eeny, meeny, miny, mo, catch a . . .' a pause was forced on me as the enormity of what I was about to say dawned. '. . . rabbit by the toe,' said Rory, completing the rhyme.

Rika, I think, would have liked to see me out of the house. She is not someone given to short telephone calls, and I was getting under her feet, but the money was holding up reasonably well – she was earning some – so redundancy wasn't too bad.

Against this idyllic background were those intrusive visits to the City for interviews. The City's (some might say quaint) mediaeval street plan permits the penetration of little actual daylight into its orifices, or even offices. Those buildings which do benefit from the direct incidence of the sun's rays shield them out with Venetian blinds, and modern architects for some reason have a preference for windows that don't open.

Two large IRA bombs have given the City fathers an exciting planning opportunity which they seem to have passed over. For a period after each bomb you could walk in certain City streets and hear the sound of footsteps. Rather nice, and something that Londoners have not experienced for nearly 100 years. In the morning, the clip of feet falling on the pavement was more purposeful, with no one talking, as the owners of the feet headed for another day of wage slavery. In the evening, the steps were slower, and people would be talking to each other on their way home. Some permanent large open green spaces with no cars would not only make the City more pleasant but would help the commercial property market, by creating a space shortage, as well as saving the government from bailing out white elephants like Canary Wharf. (It has always puzzled me that the police actually stopped a large IRA bomb going off at Canary Wharf.)

Gen called me across to a corner in the garden, where he had turned over a stone, and discovered a lot of slithering fauna. 'A good metaphor for the City,' I murmured. 'What's a metaphor, Dad?'

I was now roughly three months out of the City, and already feeling like a bit of an outsider. Meetings with committed, hard-working potential employers continued, but such people had no sparkle in their eyes. If you look at someone's eyes it is always a give away; City people, even as they tell you, with genuine enthusiasm, about dynamic thrusting strategies for opening up such and such a market, say it with joyless eyes, with no sparkle. The sparkle stays in the champagne.

I knew this, and my spell of redundancy was waking me up to LIFE. 'What's the point of working in the City if you don't get paid obscene amounts of money for it?' My failure to get a job so far was making it clear to me that the amount of money I was going to get was getting less obscene by the moment. No longer would I be vying with the Chancellor of the Exchequer on the pay front. Maybe a mere MP.

(Incidentally, who would be Chancellor of the Exchequer? There is not one in the last twenty years who has covered himself in glory – with the possible exception of Geoffrey Howe, who sensibly moved on while the going was good.)

Money can't buy you happiness, I reflected. Many of the rich are unhappy, whilst carefree alcoholics in cardboard boxes under Waterloo Bridge are footloose, fancy-free, have no responsibilities, pay no rent, mortgage or tax and are beholden to no one.

On second thoughts, this somewhat romantic view that the rich aren't happy is nonsense. Or as one grossly overpaid executive of my acquaintance in the Japanese warrant market puts it: 'I'd far prefer to be rich and unhappy, than poor and unhappy – of course, best of all is being both rich and happy.'

Almost everyone in the City starts with the idea that they would do the job for five years, then bravely jack it all in and do something worthwhile and life-enhancing, using the vast sums they had put aside to help them. There are few 'lifers', to begin with at least. The problem is that few manage the discipline of saving the money: once you have a stockbroker's mortgage and a couple of kids in private school, or develop a taste for sitting on the next table to a group of celebrities at smart West End clubs, you are trapped in a gilded cage. The effort, the risk, the stress of chucking in your job becomes too much. I consider myself lucky to have had the choice forced on me.

One of my closest friends in Tokyo, Hugh Canaway, did manage to throw it all in recently. A stock analyst at Baring Securities, he had spent the morning with a client who was fund manager to a portion of the Sultan of Brunei's billions. The fund manager was a Very Important Client. A small part of the business he could dish out would certainly help the Barings P&L, which was suffering from foolish decisions like its flashy move into an excessive amount of prime office space in a new building right at the peak of Japan's property bubble. You'd think that these stockbrokers, who make their living advising clients from Scottish widows through to the Sultanate of Brunei on how and more crucially when to invest, would avoid mistakes like this. Still, large numbers of key staff at Barings have demonstrated an understanding of selling at the top of markets – by leaving.

The man from the Sultanate had scant understanding of the principles of investment, recounts Hugh. In addition, he was monolingual, and that language was not English (or Japanese, which Hugh speaks very well). Hugh began to ask himself what he was doing with his life, going through the motions, but not being understood by this financial troglodyte, to whom he was trying to explain the intricacies of the Japanese property market. ('Very simple, sell everything you've got, you git.')

Lunchtime came. Hugh left the fund manager in the hands of the salesman, and went off to do his daily workout in the gym.

It must be something about those executive treadmills. There is no scenery, beyond, if you are lucky, admiring the bum of the girl in front, nothing to do on them except think. Hugh thought.

'Life is passing me by. Dear God, can I have another one, please?'

'No mate, that's yer lot.'

An actual parting of the clouds and accompanying thunderclap was not necessary for him to realise that this was so.

Like everyone, Hugh had resignation fantasies, and had even had thoughts as to how he would cope. 'The grass is always greener' syndrome is met by the balancing fear that once over the hedge or the hill onto that greener-looking grass, the greenness will prove to have been a snare and a delusion. Good sense – or more accurately, cowardice – usually stops that leap. At least in broking there is the compensation of being rich whilst unhappy.

Hugh, on a whim, returned from lunch and resigned, just like that. He resigned to the same bloke I'd met six years before, the one with the grown-under-a-flowerpot pallor who had assessed my character (correctly) as flippant, and wisely not employed me.

He was surprised by Hugh's action, but made no attempt to stop it. Hugh had been in Tokyo five years, and was thus very expensive to employ. It was not just his salary, but the sumptuous flat in a gaijin enclave, and the fact that the company was paying his income tax. The awkward gap between revenue and outgoings created by the move into the new office building would close fractionally.

It would be nice to think that I too had had the courage to chuck it all in. To put your life first, to put greed and money behind you, is to do something that few people have the courage to do. You could look the world in the face with a feeling of smug, sanctimonious, manly virtue: 'I am bigger than mere greed, I survived, I don't need it.' I would like to think that Hugh took his lead from me. I did it first. Nearer to the truth is that I was done first, by the commercially astute people of Merrill Lynch, who realised quite rapidly that hopes had been pinned on me incorrectly.

I had been casting around for alternatives, but in my heart of hearts, I knew I did not really want to be a widget salesman when I grew up, any more than I had originally wanted to be an equity salesman, before I had drifted aimlessly into it upon my return from Japan.

I could speak Japanese, which had to be worth something to somebody. But there was no point in abandoning the aim of being paid like a First Secretary to the Treasury, only to end up doing a dull job for half the money. It is a sad fact that most people have jobs not careers, and are dissatisfied with them in all walks of life. I once met a household name BBC presenter, in a position for which many would give their eye teeth; she was bored and looking for something new, but couldn't find it.

Completely opting out of the rat race, perhaps by buying a yacht and sailing around the world, is one solution. As a student, I made several two- or three-month trips, to places like India, Peru and China. On these trips I'd meet people who'd opted out, and gone on the road. They became objects of admiration and emulation; I too would never get caught in a rut, life was too short, I would be like them. They had spent their time visiting uplifting places, seeing colourful people, eating interesting food. If they came across somewhere particularly interesting, they could settle down for several weeks, even months, and get under its skin, perhaps having a searing beach romance with a mulatto maiden before moving on.

The trouble is though, that after the brave decision to be beholden to no man, few of them become a Paul Theroux or a Bruce Chatwin. The others somehow manage to become bored by the cycle of beautiful sights, and peoples, and of teaching English to hopeless foreign businessmen to finance the next trip.

Occasionally there is one who has kept his dignity; I met an Englishman in Bolivia whose 40kg pack contained two lead crystal wine glasses. He groaned under the weight of his belongings, but he could lay them around his room (or tent – he had one of those in there too), put up a picture or two, and call it home.

In general, such people develop obsessions with finding the cheapest hotel or exchange rate, and where to sell the whisky on the black market: arrogant about tourists as opposed to travellers, as well as the locals; in short, intolerant of their fellow man. They become bored with their freedom, which is surely a worse corruption than being bored with a highly-paid job in the City.

Rika got obvious enjoyment from her job. If the Japanese were lashing out on a documentary overseas, the team would tend to be top-notch, so she'd spend a lot of time with people at the summit of their professions, and not only in TV but in the subject areas of the documentaries she was involved in. Thus she might be out at dinner with the Director of the British Museum one evening, having spent the day filming artefacts that the public don't see, and having them explained by the world's leading authority. The next day she would be hobnobbing with Kurosawa. A bit more interesting than Merrill Lynch's market strategist.

I confess to ferocious envy of her job satisfaction, but was not too keen on the attitude towards stockbrokers that went with it. Media types, writers, artists, actors, somehow manage to occupy the moral high ground, both believing that they are doing something more worthwhile than stockbrokers or advertising execs, and being believed.

I remember going to see an excellent and moving play by homeless people (a.k.a. tramps and hooligans) with Rika and a photographer friend. I felt in the dock. Somehow I was made to feel that it was my fault that these people were homeless.

The photographer asked whether the play might change the way that I voted, which was a presumptuous question. She was a young and up-and-coming photographer, with an exhibition in some gallery for young and up-and-coming photographers. She had been to Albania, and taken pictures of hayricks there, from various different angles. I couldn't see that taking pictures of Albanian hayricks was in any way more worthwhile than shunting capital around the place. At least in theory, shunting capital has the effect of rewarding efficient companies, which then expand, creating jobs, occasionally even for homeless people. And if the brokers and investment bankers weren't doing the job reasonably efficiently, there would be no spare cash for people to go off and do things like taking pictures of Albanian hayricks; more fun, more fulfilling, maybe, but intrinsically a lot less worthwhile. People who make their living out of photographing Albanian hayricks are as parasitic as brokers or advertising execs (or writers).

I don't mean to criticise her for being a parasite. There's nothing wrong with that. My criticism is directed at the hypocrisy whereby writers, artists or alternative comedians see themselves, and indeed are seen, as morally superior to stockbrokers.

If my thinking was moving away from stocks towards widgets, or whatever, it had nothing to do with a Conversion on the Road to Damascus, of rejecting 1980s loadsamoney values. I still like money. Preferably loads of it. If I could be both well paid and contented, I would; the two are not mutually exclusive. But there was the thought nagging away that life was slipping by. Can I have another one? 'No mate, that's yer lot.'

The reader is bound to guess that part of the denouement of this book is that its writer becomes a writer.

It came to me as I was driving back from a game of cricket, in which I had scored my usual three runs and taken my usual no wickets (as well as spilling a humiliatingly easy catch). My mum had recommended to me a book about an advertising executive who had cashed in his chips and gone to live in Provence, thereby doing what every City worker, and a good few others besides, would have liked to do.

The reality for people like me was a lot harsher. For people not like me, i.e. really up against it, harsher still. I had been fired by Merrill Lynch, and couldn't get another job. That idyllic, bucolic, simple, life-enhancing life, sigh, wish I'd done that. Rather like I wish I'd ended up earning more than the Prime Minister in the City. Or hung on to some of what I did earn. Or not taken out that crazy mortgage. Or not increased it when the overdraft started to get out of hand. Or at least taken out decent redundancy insurance when the premiums were still cheap.

Most of my great thoughts occur in the car, which is awkward for a writer. People stare at me at traffic lights, talking to myself. Being in the car, and thus away from paper, most of my great thoughts get forgotten in the car too, but this one remained with me.

Life isn't like that. Virtually no one sells out at the top and moves off to live a life of bucolic simplicity and contentment in Provence. And in fact, if you read the blurb carefully, you realise that Peter Mayle gave up advertising and had been writing for fifteen years.

I would tell it as it is. Really rather pleasant actually, floating around at home doing nothing.

There is another book which gives an incorrect impression of life as it really is or was, with a City emphasis, called *Liar's Poker* by Michael Lewis. It is slightly maddening because Lewis seems genuinely to have lost the need to earn grillions and sat down to write a book. And wrote a bestseller. You'd think that one bout of success would be enough.

Hugh once introduced me to another Baring Securities stock analyst called Mark Coutts-Smith, who had also thrown it all in to do something worthwhile – in his case to help manage the overseas tours of a group of Japanese drummers. This involves living on The Isle of Sado, off Niigata in North East Japan, and being paid very little. The drummers are the practitioners of the Art of Kodo – which loosely translates as the Way of the Drum (c.f. Judo – The Gentle Way – the Japanese have always been hypocritical). They have amazing muscled torsos, which make the Chippendales look weedy, and a traditional form of Japanese jockstrap, the name of which escapes me.

Before he made his life change, Mark had once had the task of ushering Michael Lewis, in his post-broking shackle-free existence, round Tokyo, while he researched his latest book. To Mark, Mr Lewis was just another boring client, rather pleased with himself, which scarcely made him stand out from other clients. Such visitors come to Tokyo once or twice a year, and expect to be shown a good time. But if, like Mark, you have to show a good time to two or three of these people a week, the all-smiling package tour guide act palls, particularly if you are just hanging on for that mega bonus before trucking off to the Isle of Sado.

To Mark, Michael Lewis was getting in the way of a potentially productive date with a Japanese girl. Mr Lewis kept on dropping remarks like 'As I said in my book . . .' or 'I think I identified that problem in my book.' Mark was thoroughly used to clients having their own theories about things, and equally used to taking no notice of them. He failed to ask 'What book?' and then go on to say 'Are YOU the author of *Liar's Poker*?!?' with a suitably large number of exclamation marks. The author of *Liar's Poker* became visibly more irritated by the moment, possibly imagining himself to be the subject of a piss-taking exercise.

In fact, Mark was bored stupid by broking. About to join his troupe of jockstrapped drummers, he had probably made a conscious decision not to read any books about business, however funny, and had not, therefore, read *Liar's Poker*, and his broker's antennae were so ill tuned (because switched off), that he had failed to hear of it either. He has read it now, I am told, and enjoyed it (as one can't fail to), although like everyone else I know, did not get beyond page 200 of THE funny book of Wall Street, the City and the 1980s (the intricacies of the mortgage bond market finish most people off).

Mr Lewis has addressed the 200-page itch problem in his book about the Japanese economy called *Pacific Rift*. It fights slightly shy of getting to page 100. I hope Mark feels guilty for not supplying more material. I shouldn't mock: speaking as an author one of the nicest things that can happen to you is the occasional "are you THE Jim Parton?!?" moment. Way too infrequent. Much of this was going through my mind as I approached home in the car on the way back from the cricket match. Being out for a duck and taking no wickets was forgotten. I would write a book to put the record straight: most City and Wall Street people are thoroughly ordinary run-of-the-mill chaps like you (and me). Television images of young men snapping 'BUY, BUY, SELL' into three telephones simultaneously give a completely false image. Most of the time it is bloody boring.

That young man wearing a stripy shirt and bold braces, in his convertible Porsche with leather seats, in the next car along at the traffic lights undoubtedly earns three times what he is worth. If you are the envious sort, then to be told that his job is boring and he probably wants to chuck it in, will not be any compensation. Better to be rich and unhappy than poor and unhappy. Life is unfair, but the way to deal with it is to realise that his good luck is not your bad luck; it is just the way life's cookie crumbled. Envy of the good fortune of others is a very unattractive trait.

If that sounds too moralistic, then content yourself with the thought that the man has a need to flaunt his success in this way because he almost certainly has a short willy, or some other personality defect, which is why he is doing so well. He has something to prove.

Rika had been in Venice (or was it Cannes?). When she came back I told her that I was no longer going to look for jobs. She affected delight. 'You always hated broking,' she said, 'I am glad you have found something you want to do.' What else could she say, with all those friends taking meaningful pictures of Albanian hayricks? I would be becoming one of them.

22

I volunteered to become a house husband. Although the idea was treated as a joke, it wasn't meant as one. It did not appeal to Rika, possibly because of the Hermès scarf and Chanel suit dependency problem she had developed. My lack of income was making her have to be a bit more discreet about this habit. Somebody needs to found a sister organisation to Alcoholics Anonymous – Brand Names Anonymous, a bit of a contradiction in terms, admittedly.

Redundancy has its compensations: the garden, my pretty cottage, the lack of the daily grind, or that terrible feeling on Sunday evenings, with the thought of what I had failed to achieve over the all too brief weekend, the tyranny of the Sunday business pages. I was always in a BAD MOOD of a Sunday night, tense about getting to work on Monday to spend a week being unfulfilled.

But I was under Rika's feet, no question about it. The initial pleasure of seeing more of the absent spouse (if pleasure it was), and having him not in a permanent state of fatigue, was replaced by a yearning for the old freedoms and space. I'd managed not to get too despondent about my redundancy, but was probably less fun to have around than I might have been. It is probable that in similar circumstances not a few marriages bite the dust. Also, the financial noose was starting to tighten, and just as the alcoholic has his secret gin bottle, Rika had her secret Hermès catalogue.

We were having the odd row, and a lot of stony silences. At one point I did feel induced to make the jibe, 'This is not a bad time to get divorced: I'm not earning any money.'

Rika, for all her foibles, was a lovely girl. Intelligent, funny, beautiful. Intolerant, a bloody nightmare to live with.

I reflected on how I had met her. It was on a train, a forty-minute hop between Kyoto and Osaka, in about 1984. An attractive nineteen-ish girl sat next to me. I was impressed because Japanese girls tend to be a bit shy of sitting next to strange foreigners on trains. I looked over her shoulder at her diary, in which she was checking something. She had a date to go and see a film called 'An Office and a Gentleman'. As English teacher and cultural ambassador, I felt it my duty to point out to her that it ought to be 'Officer'. We got along famously, and at the end of the journey exchanged telephone numbers.

I think we rang each other once, but nothing came of it. She was busy, and couldn't be lured out for a date, and subverted by a foreigner on the make. I never quite forgot about her though.

Then I met her again quite by chance in a bookshop. We chatted for a while, and she disappeared from my life again for a few more months. But I kept on meeting her by chance, in the tube, in a department store and I found her enchanting.

I'm not a religious person, but in crowded Osaka with its ten million or so inhabitants, the odds against each chance meeting were so great that the relationship somehow began to seem 'meant'.

We began to start meeting on purpose, and it wasn't long before I was completely in love. Who knows, she may have been too.

She came to live in England, and we eventually got married at Brixton registry office when she was three months pregnant. We had no guests whatsoever, not even supportive people like my brother. It was a kind of protest at the fact that our respective parents were less than thrilled at what had happened. My parents thought she was too young (at 21) and that I was more in love with her than she with me. Her parents knew me well from Osaka days; we got on well enough, but in their ideal world she'd have married a suitable Korean, though they did acknowledge that I was a step up from a Japanese. We decided that if we couldn't celebrate it properly, we wouldn't celebrate it at all.

Our witnesses were two people plucked from the bus stop. One was a heavily pregnant black teenager. When I look at the wedding photos, I see her clutching a half-finished bottle of Lucozade. Not exactly champagne. She looked as bewildered to be pregnant as Rika. The other witness, an old lady, refused at first to be recruited, but was then quite amused by the idea. I got the impression that after a few minutes' shocked reflection at the bus stop, she got caught up in the romance of this unusual, anonymous young couple getting married alone. Rika, it must be said, was looking very exotique, in a fabulous deep pink Korean Choguri (I think that's what it's called).

And so we were married. Brixton registry office is not quite Gretna Green, but romantic enough in its way.

23

In June, Rika and Gen made their annual trip to Japan to see the grandparents. In my redundant state, I baulked at the cost and stayed at home. I still went for the odd interview, played cricket at weekends, fiddled around with the train set, drove Mr Gibbon to distraction with my piano playing and DIY. Bliss.

When you are not working, or are self-employed as I have become, and the wife is away, despite the leisure and freedom, weekends and evenings become, if anything, more important, because that is when all those dull people with proper jobs come out to play.

I began to discover a few of the pros and cons of being self-employed. The pros are obvious: complete freedom and mastery of your own destiny. Or at least you think they are obvious. The difficulty comes when you attempt to actually master that destiny. Most self-employed people are involved in an undignified scramble to get enough business to survive. This often means working far harder than you ever did as an employee, and usually for far smaller rewards.

There are also the hidden costs of self-employment, such as the need to get out in the evening, if you work from home. If you fail to do so, you can contract a form of cabin fever, from being on your own all the time, and go slightly mad. Madness is probably quite a good thing, in the correct quantities, and the right professions. You only have to look at pictures of Einstein and Beethoven, for example, to realise that these two people were off their heads, but once you examine their records in, respectively, relativity and music you realise that that this was A Good Thing.

But if you are a fine accountant say, or do what I do, namely translate Japanese Forex dealing manuals and the like into English, then these qualities of madness are not obviously advantageous. 'Concerning verification of Deutschmark/Dollar Interest Rate Arbitrage trades, attention must be paid to the Interbank Late Trade

Rule 01-03-002.' Rendering such a sentence into English can involve one's appearance passing through a Beethoven or Einstein phase as you tear your hair out, whilst working out what on earth they mean, but not caring in the slightest. My clients, unfortunately, are less understanding than Beethoven's, because sadly, I am not a genius. And in translation, even if I were a genius, it wouldn't count; you just have to be right or wrong, which is the same with a lot of freelance professions, e.g. accountancy.

This daily exposure to madness makes it essential to get out in the evening, because mad creative accountants or translators are simply not tolerated. And going out is expensive.

As Rika was away, I would ring up an old friend from teaching in Japan days, Flick. She was head of Canadian bond dealing at some Canadian Bank. I don't quite know how much she used to earn, but if I could have bought her earnings for £150,000, I would have bought large.

(Digression:

City people make markets in anything, e.g. 'She looks old. What do you think?'

'Thirty-three to thirty-four.'

'I'd buy thirty-four large.' i.e. she looks about forty or,

'I'd go short at thirty-three.'

Translation: you are being a bit harsh, she is only about thirty.)

Flick wouldn't mind me saying that many would have made a price in her age of thirty-three to thirty-four. With the benefit of insider knowledge, I would have been a seller at thirty-three (real age thirty). But the market maker would have had no difficulty jobbing my stock, sold at thirty-three, on to a buyer at thirty-four. The fact is, she looked knackered and haggard.

We would meet for a chat in a restaurant somewhere (eating whilst gabbling inconsequentially is one of the things I do best). I would complain that I couldn't get a job, while she would complain that she hated hers, and incidentally, couldn't get a boyfriend.

'Looking like that,' I would say to her – and basically she is very attractive – 'it is not surprising.'

I know Flick very well, and can say things like that, after not all that much wine.

Well before coffee, she would be showing signs of somnolence. 'Supposing, Flick, a nice boy does ask you out on a date, he is scarcely going to be impressed by your lined, grey appearance, particularly if . . .' I would pause to look theatrically at my watch, '. . . you are falling asleep at nine fifteen. This is a turn-off to men, who want at least to think that their conversation has been dazzling, and that they have a small chance, even if not this time, of getting lucky. Stress-related chain-smoking is no good either. You have got to make a decision between earning a quarter of a million a year, or getting laid. In this life, short of sleeping with your Kuwaiti clients, often you can't do both.'

Many people who get sex regularly might ignorantly opt for the quarter of a million, but I am glad to say that Flick has given up bonds and become a drama student. She looks lovelier than I have seen her in ten years. And unlike me she has got a bit of dosh stashed away.

Another letter arrived from the Merrill Lynch company car man. This too threatened the bailiffs and attendant costs if I didn't pay that parking fine. I decided not to; I wanted to see if they would really kick a man when he was down. In the event, I successfully called their bluff, thereby saving myself thirty-two pounds. Not much of a triumph in the Great Scheme of Merrill Lynch.

I had the house to myself for close on a month. While Rika was away, a letter arrived from a friend of hers, a German called Hermann. He wanted to bring his fiancée to stay. I am a known German-hater, but Rika's friends are Rika's friends. I wrote back and told Hermann the German that he could use my house as a base for sightseeing, but that I wasn't sure when Rika and Gen would be back.

Three weeks on, and they were due at some indeterminate time the next week. Indeterminate because I had tried to get in touch to no avail; she had been in Tokyo working, and August is peak

Japanese holiday season, so getting flights was a problem. By the time I did catch her, and found out when she was returning, I had committed myself to a weekend away, which I didn't feel like cancelling.

Part of the reason was that Rika's returns from solo trips to Japan were always very tense times. I had just survived (so I thought) my life crisis – hooray, I'm no longer a stockbroker – but she went through one every year. I guess that each time she came back she started to ask herself what on earth she was doing here, rather as I do whenever I come back from France to English weather, bad manners, dirt and inefficiency, somehow overlooking French dirt, bad manners and inefficiency. When she left Japan, even as a member of the unpopular, discriminated-against Korean minority, she left a world of certainties, Mum's cooking, her own futon on her own tatami, familiar smells, attitudes, the right brand of seaweed.

It took quite a man to bear the brunt of all these feelings. I was not much of a man, so I decided that although I would meet her at the airport, I would not cancel my weekend.

I wondered what stunt she would pull this time, but as a minimum I steeled myself for some, or all of the following.

1. An accusation of being unfaithful. Fat chance. If only. If those mums from the school knew what they were missing. There I was, lonely, effectively single, vulnerable; all they would have had to say was, 'Come to bed with me,' and I would have been theirs. Nothing remotely like this ever occurred

2. A new, disciplined child-rearing routine; this was the mark of an over-fastidious mother-in-law. There would be new stringent standards of hygiene – I was brought up to eat my toast if it fell on the floor, even butter side down; this taught me not to drop my toast butter side down on the floor, besides doing wonders for my immune system. The Japanese as a people are appalling hypochondriacs, consuming more medicines per capita than any other people on earth (Data:

Merrill Lynch). Gen would be dressed up in expensive clothes; Japanese ones are excellently made, and so long as I didn't pay for them, I didn't care what they cost, but they were a bit foppish for my tastes. As the main Gen handler, I would be under constant pressure to keep them clean and creased in the right places, and this was something that I couldn't be bothered with, or even approve of. All children's (boys' and girls') clothes should be able to withstand climbing up a tree for example, without having to be sent to the dry cleaners afterwards.

3. Jet lag made bed sharing, making noise at 11 a.m. etc., a source of massive tension.

4. Rika's employers, having been reminded of her existence by a personal visit to Tokyo HQ, would besiege her with faxes and telephone calls in the middle of the night and make unreasonable demands on her time. They, no more than her parents, could never remember whether to add or to subtract eight hours when calling England, with devastating impact on domestic harmony. This would make her more grumpy and prone to caprices.

The option of disappearing for the weekend rather than looking after my returning wife may seem uncaring but, in both our interests, it was obvious.

When I went to Heathrow, Gen at least, was delighted to see me, and yabbered away at me in Japanese about his holiday. In England he would stop me speaking Japanese, I think he found the damage I inflicted on its grammar too painful, but just being back he was in tolerant mood.

'Baba and Jiji (Granny and Grandpa) can't speak English, so I have to talk to them in Japanese,' he said proudly. 'You can't speak Japanese, so I have to speak to you in English,' he went on, in Japanese, clearly not noticing which one he was using.

The lucky little sod, able to pick it up like that, without any effort. I am often asked 'How did you pick up Japanese?' This is a specious question, because the Japanese language is not one that Europeans 'pick up'. You do that to Japanese girls. In fact, I swotted very hard for three years, have been using it for seven, and am still at a level that would never be tolerated in a 'fluent' translator of French, say.

He was lucky too, having parents who made him speak both; inevitably English had proved dominant, because that is what was spoken by the likes of Rory, but he had enough Japanese so that a visit to Japan of one month would bring it all out.

I wanted to take Gen away for the weekend, it would protect Rika, and she could go through all her funny moods on her own, including the annual appraisal of whether or not she had messed up her life completely in marrying a wog like me. This process would no doubt be worse this year, because I had decided that the personal cost of earning lots in the City was no longer worth it. For her, this would imply the H.A.V. virus going firmly into remission.

Children don't appear to get jet lag in quite the same way. With no sense of time, they don't have the built-in self-fulfilling expectation that they are not going to be able to go to sleep.

Rika wouldn't let me take him, and, as stated above, there was no point in arguing when the wife had just got off an aeroplane.

I spent an agreeable few days away. I decided I might as well not rush back, but allow Rika to adjust to her new bedtime, and the horror of being in England, alone. I tried to ring her a couple of times, but only got my own voice on the answerphone.

I returned home from my weekend on Wednesday evening. There was no one there, which was a disappointment, and a bit strange; I had been looking forward to seeing them both fully recovered. In the sink there were the usual unwashed mugs and plates, and there were toast crumbs on the table. Proof, if I needed it, that she was back, and that my mother-in-law's standards hadn't all rubbed off, or were short lived. Always a relief.

An empty wine bottle was evidence either of an attempt to readjust to the time zones through alcohol, or of revelry. I listened to the messages on the answerphone, which shifted the weight of evidence towards revelry. What could she have been celebrating?

It was a funny time of day to be out and not to have left a message. Upstairs the mystery deepened. The bed was unmade, which was not unusual, and there were a few dirty clothes dotted around the place, but the normal array of Clinique, L'Oreal, her favourite Diorissimo, was not on the Victorian armoire. The fax machine didn't have five feet of Japanese characters spilling out of it. Indeed the fax machine had gone. In its place was a new £6.99 Dixons telephone. An envelope was sellotaped to it, with 'Jim' written on the outside.

> Dear Jim,
>
> I have decided that it is time to face up to things. Our marriage is not working. I have decided to go away for a period to think things over. I will be in touch shortly. Be patient, and don't worry.
>
> Speak to you soon, Lots of Love, Rika

My first reaction was that this was par for the course, shortly after a return from Japan, when homesickness did weird things to her. Perhaps I shouldn't have stayed away for so long, but been on hand to wait and serve, and endure the slings and arrows of outrageous jet lag.

It was true that we hadn't been getting on all that well. I'd been under her feet for several months, and I am not the greatest exploiter of the acres of free time available to me. I might, for example, have studied for and taken those stock exchange exams, or other qualifications I had successfully avoided acquiring when actually working. Moping indolently around the house, overplaying 'Für Elise' – always getting stuck on the same bit – bashing tacks into either a train set or the floor, or suddenly deciding to redesign the kitchen. With hindsight, I can see that I must have been infuriating to live with (and indeed next door to).

But she'd just had a one-month respite from that, and in any case, trips to Venice and Cannes, and evenings out with visiting production crews meant that we were like ships passing in the night. We hadn't been seeing much of each other at all.

I racked my brain to think where she might have gone. She had a million and one acquaintances from work, of all nationalities and in all countries, to whom she might be able to go, and I wouldn't have the first idea of where to start looking.

Address books, diaries, important papers, the majority of her underwear, charcoal-grey and mattress ticking Issey Miyake sack dresses, Chanel suit and other favourite clothes were all gone. Gen's drawer didn't have any foppish clothes in it either. The only remaining Hermès scarf had a dribble of red wine down one corner (i.e. was unwearable). I started to become more worried. This was serious.

Perhaps my first thought should have been for Rika, my wife, but it was for Gen. Once in Japan, extracting Gen would be very difficult. The law is very expensive and very slow. He'd be a teenager, and I a pauper, before I got him out, if I ever did. I had visions of renting a yacht, sailing into Kobe then bribing a Yakuza, a Japanese mafia man, to kidnap Gen and bring him to my boat at the dead of night. We'd then set sail through typhoons to Hong Kong, be swept ashore on an uninhabited volcanic outcrop, be boarded by Filipino pirates, Gen would be sold into white (well, yellowish) slavery, my message in a bottle picked up by a passing yacht piloted by a (James Bond-type) girl with large almond shaped eyes and a tattoo, we'd run the gamut of Triad motor launches, sinister Chinese communist drug smugglers, fall in love, blah, blah, blah. The plot of my first novel.

The yakuza would have to find out where Gen lived first though. I remembered a student of English of mine whose father had disappeared; divorce was too cumbersome a procedure, it was much simpler just to vanish amongst the thirty million people living in Tokyo and Yokohama.

I pictured myself surveilling the wife's house. Six feet four, fair hair. Dark glasses and a bottle of dye would not solve the problem of passing incognito. I resolved that I had no choice but to stay calm.

The answerphone messages and the wine bottles pointed to a party. I went outside to the dustbins and sifted through some of the rubbish, not a pleasant job in mid-August. Champagne bottles! Bollinger at that. Decaying sushi! Korean chicken! Forensic evidence pointed unerringly towards some kind of celebration.

24

Several days passed, and no message came. Mutual friends had no idea, so I stopped calling them. In any case it was embarrassing, unmanly even, to have to admit to having mislaid one's wife.

I racked my brain for the names of some of her friends, but the problem was that I couldn't remember their surnames.

Talking of friends, Hermann the German rang to say that he and his fiancée Marlene would be leaving Edinburgh and hoped to come and stay tomorrow. Fine I said. If Rika phoned in, it might shame her into a reappearance.

To take my mind off things I busied myself with a round of frantic gardening and lawn grooming designed to irritate Mr Gibbon. I mastered the slow movement of the 'Pathétique Sonata'.

A couple of days later, a letter arrived from Bartrip, Bowles, and Bartrip Solicitors at Law, saying that Rika and Gen were fine, staying with friends and would be in touch soon.

I went through as many of Rika's papers as I could find. I came across a letter from a friend of hers, Jennifer: 'I don't blame you for wanting to leave Jim. If there is anything at all I can do to help, don't hesitate to ask . . .' The letter was two years old. I wondered what I had done to engender such disapprobation.

I had always quite liked Jennifer, but the relationship had been an uneasy one. It was something to do with my having been a stockbroker, probably. There was that knee-jerk disapproval. She was doing a Ph.D. in some branch of cognitive linguistics. I couldn't see that was any more worthwhile than photographing Albanian hayricks, and considerably less worthwhile than broking stocks, or indeed, being a currency speculator and knocking Britain out of the ERM.

When Gen was small, I once rugby tackled him on the drawing room carpet. 'He's going to be a rugby player when he grows up,' I said proudly to the assembled company of students, one of whom was Jennifer.

There was an almost unified bristling round the room. 'Maybe he'll be very good at knitting,' said Jennifer, putting into words a thought clearly shared by a number of the women present. Her sons would obviously be given black Barbie dolls to play with. Or perhaps Ken and close companion, with His and His smoking jackets. Personally I didn't feel that it was important to argue as to whether Gen's potential lay in knitting or rugby. In due course he would find out for himself. For me, it was not an issue upon which to bristle.

I continued my search through Rika's belongings, not a nice thing to do, but this departure was beginning to look like more than her usual bout of jet lag associated madness after a return from the land of the rising yen to the land of the sinking pound.

There was a fairly complete archive of letters going back five or six years, including all my old love letters to her, which I took and hid. There was an account of the birth of Gen written by both of us.

Rika: 5.00 a.m.: Same as usual. Jim snoring.

6.00 a.m.: Every ten minutes. Jim snoring.

7.00 a.m.: Every seven to eight minutes. Jim still snoring.

8.00 a.m.: Every five minutes. Jim got up but didn't believe.

8.30 a.m.: Jim in blind panic, but made breakfast – duck egg and sausage. (I wonder why we had duck eggs in the fridge.)

9.00 a.m.: Ate breakfast. Delicious. Every four to five minutes. Jim rang up hospital and go!

12.35 p.m.: Start delivering/push.

About 12.50 p.m.: Swap Carmen (black) for Rhona (Scottish). Too many students.

Jim: I asked Carmen if this was the real thing, because we had had not a few false alarms over the last week or two. 'Yes', she said, 'this is the real thing'.

Carmen was comforting and reassuring. Rhona who, sweet though she was, looked only about nineteen, and 'just needed one more birth to get her certificate,' brushed Carmen aside. That's the trouble with teaching hospitals. All was confusion, and though I say it myself, I reckon I took over, although Rika might disagree. I deserve the certificate.

Rika: 1.20 p.m.: I began to understand when + how to push.

1.25 p.m.: Head was seen.

1.34 p.m.: Finished.

Jim: First saw a little tuft of black hair around 11.30, when Carmen searched with her fingers. About 1.10 each push revealed a little medallion of head, which then disappeared. At 1.20 the circle of head began to get bigger and bigger. The midwife threatened the forceps. Whispers of various unpleasant sounding procedures. No one in charge it seemed. Looked around for Carmen, but there was only Rhona who was looking tense.

Told Rika I could see head each time she pushed. (Slight lie.)

1.25: Crown began to appear, until soon half the head was out. The only time Rika screamed. I encouraged her 'push' and in a few more goes the head was out. Didn't really see because she had her feet on my shoulders for pushing.

Head slimy, lots of black hair.

Cord round neck, so Rhona, relieved to be doing something, cut it, then pulled the rest of the baby out, or Rika pushed it, I can't remember.

Blue, slimy baby on Rika's chest, she seemed a bit bewildered, both crying a bit.

Rika: Jim gave me nice rub + kept telling me what was happening + how to do. Jim said, 'It's a boy, Rika'. I found him on my stomach. Colour is blue and purple. Soon went pink. I saw his big hands in front of my eyes. I could imagine his feet, of course. (An unkind reference this to the proud father's size thirteens.)

I got on with life. I couldn't sit around moping at home, so I applied myself to gardening, listening to the cricket commentary on the radio, bashing in a few stray tacks.

It wasn't until Wednesday, a whole week after her disappearance, that Rika finally got in touch and we were able to meet. In the meantime I had got myself a solicitor to combat hers.

Rika seemed in very good humour when I met her in Soho Square. Her manner was slightly euphoric – 'I've done it,' it seemed to say. She had leapt the hedge to the greener grass on the other side. I recognised the symptoms. I felt the same when I decided to give up broking.

Her manner was pleasant, sympathetic, kind even, but she wouldn't tell me where she was staying, or what she planned.

Our hour in Soho Square drew to a close. Round us sat hundreds of lunchtime sun seekers, secretaries with their skirts pulled up to their thighs, defying warnings about the ozone layer, catching a few end-of-summer rays, or forty winks, or eating their sandwiches. Darren the office boy was out with Sharon the office girl, catching a furtive half-hour of untramelled staring into each other's eyes. Life continuing, while our trivial domestic soap opera played itself out.

Rika stroked my forehead and gave me a kiss before leaving. An onlooker would have taken us for a version of Darren and Sharon, a little love scene between a beautiful olive-skinned oriental girl and a tall suntanned man (never mind that the suntan was from a summer's enforced leisure and loafing about), the look of regret in the man's eyes only because the couple couldn't stay together for longer.

Rika's decision mirrored my own – I was packing in broking, she was packing in me.

I could rationalise redundancy; it was the fault of the approaching collapse of the Japanese financial system, Merrill Lynch's lack of commitment to the long term, the fact that Alick my boss, was a bastard – any number of factors other than my own inadequacies. When the wife leaves, one has to face up to the possibility that one's inadequacies may have something to do with it. Or, if it was her inadequacies, then I was inadequate for not having spotted them.

25

While I was in Soho Park, a message had been deposited on the answerphone.

Hermann the German would be coming to stay the day after tomorrow, with his new East German fiancée. My troubles had made me forget about those two.

I had only met Hermann once before, and technically speaking he was my errant wife's friend. He was a nice clean-cut Berliner of about twenty-eight, just finishing his sociology degree. (It seems that degrees take about ten years in Germany.) A typical modern-day Kraut, uncontroversial, sincere, thought that world peace and saving the environment were good things. Why anyone should imagine that the Germans could once again become a threat to Europe is beyond me. There is no shortage of out and out fascists in Germany, of course, but it is complacent of the British to look across at them (or the French) and pat ourselves on the back for our superior record of tolerance. We have just never been put under test, that's all, although maybe it is significant that Boris Becker wants to live in England with his black wife, because he believes we Brits are more tolerant.

The two arrived a few days later, and were a good distraction from my marital problems.

Marlene was from East Berlin. It was typical of Hermann's sincerity to embrace the ideals of the Nineties and go for an Easterner. To think that only a few years before their love might have led to them being shot. Forbidden fruit is the sweetest, even when obviously reared on too much kartoffel salad like Marlene.

Marlene could speak no English, and my German was limited to '*Dass ist eine shöne Pickelhaube*,' and '*Ich bin ein Berliner*', so Hermann became full-time interpreter.

As a gift to me for having them to stay, I was presented with a small marble plinth with a piece of coloured plaster on top: 'Berlin Wall, 1962-1989.' It sits on my mantelpiece still, a small symbol of optimism for the future.

Over the next few days, they embarked on a round of sightseeing: the Changing of the Guard, Tower Bridge, Madame Tussauds, a trip out of town to Windsor Castle.

Hermann was still the bright, sincere, fundamentally dull Hun he had always been. Marlene, being only eighteen months out from behind the Wall was very different in character; she had wanted to take tea at the Ritz, but they had been turfed out because of Hermann's lack of a jacket or a tie, although she had been smartly dressed enough, in a pleated skirt, demurely over the knee.

It was ironic that Hermann the Westerner should be caught in this way, rather than Marlene. I remember a trip to the Opera in the pre-revolutionary Prague of 1986. I was a stinking traveller off the Trans-Siberian train from China, with dirty Taiwanese tennis shoes, dirty (and smelly) everything, in fact. I had assumed that I would therefore fit in with the proletarian Czech audience, but in fact they were starchily formal, all in jackets and ties, and looked at me askance, as disapprovingly as the Ritz had at Hermann. I wasn't chucked out, only because I had given the usher a US dollar.

Marlene hadn't quite got the hang of dressing like a capitalist, though. There was something peculiarly totalitarian about her hairstyle, the over-bright, we-are-not-communists-anymore lipstick. But then perhaps I shouldn't be too disparaging; Hermann was dressed like a Seventies pop star.

In the middle of their stay, Rika phoned in again, and I went to meet her. The fact that I was looking after two of her friends despite being a known German-hater elicited thanks but no more. 'Send my regards to Hermann.'

We met again in Soho Square, and I am afraid that we had a humdinger argument.

She pointed out that I had once said that it would be a good time to get divorced, while I was redundant, because it would cost me less money. This was true, but I had not been expecting to be taken at my word.

Hermann and Marlene were embarrassed to be staying at a time of peak marital discord, but I said that it was not their problem and told them to relax.

Like my wife, they took me at my word. They abandoned sightseeing for a day to unwind at home.

Hermann was so relaxed that he was under the impression that it was acceptable to import some of his Northern European habits to the UK and wander the garden in his jockey briefs/pouch. He was quite slim for a German but nonetheless, rather pale and weedy, certainly no Chippendale, not quite Master Race.

Marlene's figure was a bit more stereotypically Prussian, as befits the product of a country where socialist prudery had been the norm, and therefore bodies predominantly covered. She wore a shocking-pink bikini, which struggled manfully to retain escaping flesh, but, like the Berlin Wall, was not quite up to the job. I am sure that I caught sight of the lucky Mr Gibbon diving back behind his curtains having got an eyeful, no doubt wondering what the Cold War had been about. There was some nice crumpet out East.

Like her lipstick, the bikini said, 'I-am-no-longer-a-drab-Communist-I-embrace-the-West.' Lucky old Hermann. I was sorry to see the two of them go. I hope that for the sake of a united Germany, people like Marlene don't lose their sense of irony and cynicism, and that they don't end up as over-sincere but harmless Eurobores like Hermann.

26

At the end of the third week of her flight, Rika finally came home. The threatened move to a flat had proven more difficult to execute than she had imagined.

Back too, came the fax machine, and the full armoury of other office equipment, plus calls in the middle of the night from Tokyo. Term restarted, and I resumed the merry routine of the previous six months, of ferrying Gen, who of course was delighted to see me again, to and from school.

Rika and I circled each other in the house uneasily, not having rows, but not talking either. Gen didn't seem to notice at all. He was used to us both doing separate things, but however foul we were being to each other, he was never happier than on the occasional meals we all took together.

A couple of months passed. When she was not out living it up, she tended to be in her room with the door closed. There were a lot of muffled telephone calls, the Japanese cooking knives (much better than Sabatier) started to disappear, and bit by bit, the office equipment started to shift out again. I should have been on my guard, but when you don't want to believe something, you don't believe it.

Similarly, I ought to have read the signs of my approaching demise at Merrill Lynch, such as the interviews with a Danish stockbroker about whom Alick, Henry and Charlie were very enthusiastic, and for whom, without major upheavals, there would be no place to sit.

A pleasant November morning came. As usual I got Gen up. He'd gone to bed late, so it was a delicate operation. Tickle the feet until the first signs of consciousness begin to appear, then retreat. Rika lay on in bed, awake, but making no signs of a move. Lord knows why it wasn't me agitating for divorce.

Gen was awake. Once those eyes start to flicker there was no going back. 'Good morning, Gen, did you have a nice sleep? You've got to go to school. Quick. Breakfast.'

We raced up the street. One good thing about Gen was that he liked a race, which meant that he was less late than he might be. He would get very upset if I won, but the trick was to allow him to breast the tape fractionally ahead. We passed Rory, who was creating a bit about going to school. Rory shot Gen as he went past who turned round and shot back. Rory received a welt from his mother. Corporal punishment, not exactly politically correct. 'We don't like guns, Rory,' she said. 'We like guns don't we Daddy?' said Gen. Mrs Rory looked at me disapprovingly, so I had to whisper my agreement when we were a good distance past. I think Mrs Rory probably disapproved of racing to school. Competition is bad.

I couldn't see any point in prohibiting guns, because it was impossible. As a result of a ban on firearms in Rory's house, he spent his whole time constructing them out of Lego, drawing them, even fashioning sculptures of them out of his fish fingers and instant mashed potato. (Rory's Mum, being a New Woman, couldn't be bothered to cook, a double standard, because New Men are expected to have these accomplishments.)

By the time I returned, Rika was unaccountably up, and unaccountably agitated, but then she was always unaccountably agitated. She left in a hurry saying she would be back to take Gen out to lunch with a friend.

I busied myself with tearing down the spent tomato plants and withered lobelias. There was no escaping the fact that winter was upon us. The garden was smothered with crisp brown leaves.

Lunchtime came and I had to drag Gen out of Rory's house as the two of them hid on the way back from school. I had to deliver the child to his mother so that she could take him to lunch with the friend.

'Where are you going?' I asked.

'To a Japanese restaurant, with Jennifer,' she replied.

'All right for some,' I said, thinking of the expense of Japanese restaurants and of our steadily accruing overdraft.

I had my lunch, did a bit more gardening, but was driven indoors by the cold wind and impending darkness – winter was nearly here, summer time had just ended. It had been a lovely morning, but those short afternoons are depressing. No wonder so many Swedes commit suicide in winter.

I retreated upstairs to attack a mountain of bills, and correspondence that I had been putting off for a while. My filing system has three trays, one labelled 'In', one 'Out' and one 'Procrastinate'. In practice, the 'In' tray is not substantially different in function from the 'Procrastinate' one.

Telephone bill, £1,273.58. Final reminder in red. My mum gets in trouble if the quarterly phone bill reaches fifty pounds. The secret of staying married for forty years. Around a quarter to five the front door bell rang. 'Ah Rika has forgotten her keys, or had her handbag stolen again,' I thought.

At the door was a man clad from head to foot in black leathers, clutching a motorbike helmet. Our street was built in a funny order, with a modern housing estate on one side, a row of nice Georgian stuff, then a few oddments like my house, a Thirties development built on land sold off at the back of the big Victorian house on the parallel street. This meant that the numbers were all out of order. My house, Number Fifty-three, was next to Number Six, so although I was not expecting a visit from a motorcyclist, I was not entirely surprised, and readied myself to explain to him how to find his way to Number Twenty-two.

'Are Mr Parton?' I reeled in surprise, at such a question.

'Why, yes I am.'

'Any relation to Dolly? Here mate, could you sign for these, please.' Surely the Merrill Lynch car man had given up on that unpaid parking fine. A fat brown package with my name on the outside and the legend BY HAND. Six months since I left Merrill's, it seemed to me to be taking a sledgehammer to crack a nut. I signed and took the papers.

I was right to think that it was from lawyers. Not Merrill Lynch's lawyers, my wife's.

There were twelve pages or so of tight script telling her life story, with particular emphasis on her marriage to me, and a compelling account of what a hopeless husband and rotten father I was.

I was described as potentially violent, and the train set upstairs was singled out as an example of an irresponsible attitude to safety, which I was unable to appreciate. This from a woman who couldn't even change a plug.

I had heard of the solicitor's firm concerned from reading about the divorce of one of the Royal Family. Typical of Rika to go for a brand name in divorce. Typical of them, paid by the hour, to take statements on train sets.

I suppose I must have conveyed an impression of slight madness by the look in my eyes each time I rerailed a derailed Thomas the Tank Engine.

The penultimate paragraph was a long explanation about her new flat and her hunt for new schools. In the middle of this was the sentence 'I eventually left the matrimonial home on the 4th November'.

Until this point I had been increasingly numbed by the 'Affirmation of the Petitioner', and that a relationship with someone I had loved, still loved for all her faults, (and no doubt mine) could come to this.

The 4th November. Today. She was gone. Gone with Gen. They weren't out to lunch at all. They were gone and wouldn't be back. I paced the house in a futile, impotent way, angry at being duped.

A court hearing was scheduled for just three days later. I went to the school to explain the situation. I had bottled my emotions until then, but there was something about going through that Victorian gate marked BOYS next to the one marked INFANTS that set me off. I bit my upper lip, projected it, stiffened it, but it was no good. I cried.

I took some deep breaths, and walked around the empty playground. Children's voices could be heard coming from the classrooms, and the odd, more strident one of a Joyce Grenfell-like teacher. I went into the nursery bit, composed.

I talked to Gen's teacher, who was astonished to find that there were any problems between myself and my wife. 'He seems such a well-adjusted child,' she said. This set me off again, and the teacher had to take me outside, while Rory, momentarily distracted from the creation of a plasticine gun, remarked to his chums with a child's devastating bluntness, 'Gen's Daddy's crying.' I expect they all went home and told their mums. Quite exciting.

A few days later my solicitor, barrister and I formed up at the Royal Courts of Justice in the Strand, the one you always see on the Nine O'Clock News. A fabulous Victorian Gothic monster, it seemed extraordinary such facilities could be available to help us solve our menial domestic squabble. Our court was in an annex with a massive vaulted corridor for litigants to wait in. Everyone talked in subdued whispers. You could tell who the lawyers were because they all looked so relaxed, and the lady solicitors and barristers were all dressed in black. Despite this, another male lawyer came up to me to ask me how long I thought my client's case would take. I indicated my lawyers, both female. 'Sexist,' they muttered as the male lawyer retreated.

With the benefit of hindsight, I can add the epithet 'stupid', because I have subsequently discovered that the overwhelming majority of matrimonial lawyers are women.

I saw Rika on the other side of the corridor, with her lawyers. Her solicitor was young and pretty, normal looking. The kind I might ask for a date, if we really did get divorced. It was difficult to reconcile her appearance and the horrors written about me in the 'Affirmation of the Evidence of the Petitioner'. I couldn't believe that Rika had thought all those things up. Ghastly though I may be, she must have needed some help from a more creative person. Lots of hours at £130 each had gone into the creation of that document.

I was dying to test the vaulted acoustics, and thought to myself that Gen would have loved this place. It might well have a better echo than the inside of Tutankhamun's tomb. I wondered where he was.

After waiting all morning, we were told at one o'clock that we could go to lunch, without missing our turn in the queue, as the courts adjourn for lunch. I didn't feel like eating so went for a walk on my own down by the Thames.

Back at the court, two o'clock passed, then three. The numbers of tense-looking litigants and their smart, relaxed lawyers dressed in funereal black gradually thinned out. Every so often, the door of one or other of the courts would open and one party would emerge looking upset, and in tears, and the other side would come out looking joyous and exuberant, and embrace waiting family and friends. The lawyers would look professionally indifferent.

The building was overheated, and I went for a walk in the courtyard. 'I am just going outside and may be some time,' I said to my solicitor. By the time I got back it was four o'clock and my lawyers were scouring the lavatories and the courtyards for their errant client. We were on.

The courts pack it in at 4.30 p.m., so we only had half an hour, but our case was so cut and dried that any judge would be able to come to the right decision very quickly. I shouldn't have been tense, but I was, as the barristers went through the formalities and the judge read the affidavits while we sat in you-could-hear-a-pin-drop silence for ten minutes.

4.10 p.m. Each barrister made a brief deposition on our behalf.

4.20 p.m. The other side had said in the corridor outside that if they lost, Rika would move back in with me. This was meant as a threat, but to me it was the best solution. You can't just chuck away five years of marriage that casually. She had made her point. I would try harder. I might even look for a job.

The judge looked at her watch. 'I'm afraid you can't expect me to rule on this today,' she said, 'the issues need to be heard, I will therefore adjourn this hearing until 22nd November. Time, half a day.' She ruled that I should be allowed to see Gen from after school on Fridays and that he should return to his mother at 10 a.m. on Sundays.

It was shocking to think that I could be in contempt of court if I attempted to see Gen.

I had been confident of winning, would have been unsurprised if I had lost, but a goalless draw was the last outcome I had anticipated. There seems to me a fundamental rule of life; nothing you anticipate ever happens as you'd expect. No scenario I had imagined for the outcome of the case encompassed sitting around in the court corridors for a day and having nothing decided at all.

Guessing scenarios invariably fails, because there are too many variables in the activities of men. If I extrapolate my experience in court to cover the City, or the BBC weather room for that matter, or anything else, it should send a dire warning to any would-be forecaster that forecasting doesn't work, which is why City forecasters and Chancellors of the Exchequer ought to give up trying, and the entire broking and fund management industry is a rip off.

At home there was a big void. No more friendly routine of to-ing and fro-ing from school, or visits to Rory's house. I performed some therapeutic tidying of scrumpled pyjamas, and Gen's unmade bed left over from when they had left on Monday.

Treading on Lego in bare feet on the way to the loo in the depths of the night is one of the pains of parenthood, but the fact that the child who had dropped it was no longer there gave it an additional twist.

On the two intervening patches of staying access, Gen was in good form, obviously delighted to see me. He did not understand what was going on. He had been told that he was visiting 'Mummy's work', and asked me if I wanted to come and see it. Everything was a bit of an adventure for him.

27

Two weeks later we were back in the vaulted corridor with its untested acoustics.

Again, lunchtime came and went. This time I made a show of being more relaxed, although I was feeling more tense than I had ever felt in my whole life, a tension made worse by the fact that it was a situation over which I had no control. It was down to my lawyers.

The two opposing teams sat at different ends of the corridor, avoiding each other's eyes. Every so often the two barristers would meet in the middle for a parley. Each trip to the loo involved passing the enemy dugout and making a decision as to whether to nod in acknowledgement, or look the other way. Both of us were no doubt conscious that we were employing professionals to do our dirty work for us, and internally felt rather embarrassed.

I ostentatiously affected calm, by reading the newspaper and *Private Eye*. Half past two. Half past three. Other groups slipped in ahead of us. Some were very quick, just ten minutes or so, but the group of people immediately in front of us were obviously having a real ding-dong battle.

At about a quarter to four, I popped across the road to the newsagent again, and bought six toffee bars, in the hope that Sod's Law would make the case start in my absence, as last time. This shows a scant understanding of the operations of Sod's Law. The whole point of it is that the Law's immutable action only works to thwart anything you plan. The Norman Lamont or City economist effect. If you anticipate one thing then something else happens. This meant that when I came back, no one was scouring the lavatories and courtyards for me. (Scouring in the sense of 'looking for'. I am not a lavatory cleaner.)

I kept one toffee bar for myself, and distributed one each to my lawyers. I then sauntered across to the opposition's table and slipped them one each too, then retreated. I wanted to present them with a dilemma. If they spurned them they would look churlish, if they ate them they would be communing at the table of the enemy. I wished I had thought of giving them orange ice lollies (the building was still very overheated), which would have made the dilemma more pressing because of the tendency of ice lollies to melt. I had images of my wife's young barrister pompously proclaiming in court with a bright-orange mouth.

Just short of four o'clock the court doors swung open and the previous case came out. A scuffle broke out between the, presumably, divorcing parties. I had witnessed a real life courtroom scuffle as described regularly in *The Sun*. They were called back in again to be fined for contempt of court.

Yet again it was just past four, and only half an hour before the judge packed it in for the day. My heart sank. At this rate we would soon be entering a third replay followed by a penalty shoot-out.

If the previous judge had not had time to make a decision on the basis of the affidavits alone, at four in the afternoon, neither would this one. Sure enough, he adjourned the hearing, but with a variation. He sent for the Court Welfare Officer. Not a creature I'd ever heard of before.

Fifteen minutes or so later, a kindly looking man in his mid-forties arrived and sat in the witness box while the judge explained to him the positions of the two parties. 'Redundant stockbroker . . . works from home . . . claims he has the time to look after the child . . . freelance television producer . . . says she can pick and choose jobs to fit around mothering commitments . . .' The judge ordered the man to visit our respective homes and do an assessment of whether it would be in the child's best interests to stay with the mother, or return to the father.

'Surely,' said the Court Welfare Officer, 'since we are only talking about interim care and control, shouldn't we just allow the boy to stay with his mother until a fuller hearing?'

This was certainly a worrying suggestion, but fortunately the judge disagreed. The CWO was to visit both our homes, write his report, and we would reconvene under the same judge at the beginning of December.

The CWO looked like the kind that spends his Saturday afternoons jotting down numbers at the end of Platform Four, on Reading station, so I reckoned on influencing him positively. On the other hand, as a social worker, he was certain to be left-wing, with an instinctive hatred of capitalist pig-dog stockbroker types like me. I would have to invite sympathy on account of my redundancy. On the downside, my wife would be able to play the racial minority card.

We filed out of court, and the opposition thanked me loudly for their sticky chocolate bars, and ate them ostentatiously. For them this result was the second best thing to an outright victory. It bought time. The case would not be heard before a month after the departure of Rika and Gen, and the status would have become more quo.

28

I pondered my tactics.

The day before the Court Welfare Officer's visit, two days before we were due back in court, my mum came round and scrubbed the house from top to bottom. She even cleaned the light switches, something I would never have had the imagination to do. By the end the house was gleaming.

I had kept a load of Gen's washing back, so that when the CWO came round I would have an array of clothing on the line, in order to look both domesticated and caring. City-slicker stripes and double cuffs would be suppressed.

I also stopped buying the *Daily Telegraph* for a few days and got the *Guardian* instead, with its supplements. Bit of a Fascist paper, the *Guardian*, controlled as it is by the thought police, but it is well written, and does have some useful supplements. *Guardian Society*, that was the one, and by good chance it had an article headlined, 'Increasingly Fathers Run the Home, While Mothers Win the Bread, by our Social Affairs Correspondent'. I left it carelessly but ostentatiously open by the sofa. A subliminal message would be delivered: I-used-to-be-a-stockbroker-but-I-am-all-right-now.

I felt confident but not overconfident.

The great day came. I went to pick up Gen from his new school, but he wasn't there. The judge had said that I should pick him up early to settle him down. Eventually Rika and Gen arrived. She said he had a cold and had had to go to the doctor; he looked perfectly all right to me.

I had to rush home to meet the Court Welfare Officer, leaving not enough time to bribe Gen with a McDonalds. Sharp lawyers my wife had.

The kindly looking Mr O'Rourke arrived at the front door a quarter of an hour late. The house was spotless. We chatted amiably for a couple of hours. He didn't ask me at all about the relationship I have with Gen, who played quietly upstairs with the train set. I presumed that that was taken as read.

Mr O'Rourke took the clothes line bait hook, line and sinker. 'Ah,' he said, 'I see you have some of Gen's clothes on the line.' I felt I had made a good impression. Later, he saw the copies of the *Guardian* artlessly left in various strategic locations around the house. 'Ah,' he went again, 'a stockbroker who reads the *Guardian*, how unusual.'

We empathised.

'A redundant stockbroker, Mr O'Rourke,' I replied, 'one's perspectives change.'

I gave Mr O'Rourke some tea and shortbread, slightly conscious that this was a risky strategy. Rika would subject him to a full-blown Tea Ceremony. She had also nicked all the best china.

Gen was at his most infectiously droll over tea. 'Pass Mr O'Rourke the shortbread, Gen.'

'Pass Mr O'Rourke the shortbread, Gen.'

'No, pass it, Gen.'

'No, pass it, Gen.'

'Stop copying me, and pass him the shortbread.'

'Stop copying me, and pass him the shortbread.' A little grin appeared on his face.

'This is one of Gen's favourite games, Mr O'Rourke, he loves copying me . . .'

'This is one of Gen's favourite games, Mr O'Rourke, he loves copying me.' By now Gen was laughing.

'If you don't stop copying me, I'll . . .' I paused at the looming disaster. Social worker Mr O'Rourke would certainly not approve of smacking bottoms.

'If you don't stop copying me, I'll . . .' The little swine had the intonation perfectly, right down to the hint of desperation.

Apart from this small incident, Gen behaved impeccably throughout, and the Court Welfare Officer and I, I felt, parted on the best of terms.

There was one small incident, just before he left, which perhaps could have been better choreographed. Mr O'Rourke professed an interest in music, and so I gave him a little rendition on the piano.

His chest puffed out an inch or so as he ventured confidently 'J. S. Bach?'

'C.P.E. Bach,' I replied, too quickly. You might have thought that I would be immune to such errors, after five years of sucking up to my clients in the City. No wonder I lost my job.

His report dropped on my doormat a few days later. He'd obviously relished the multi-ethnic nature of his task, pointing out in his report that 'Gen' was spelt with a hard 'g'. It said, that 'Mr Parton, whilst obviously a caring father, is not, in my opinion, capable of looking after the child on a full-time basis . . . the child also exhibited some provocative behaviour in his presence which he did not, at any rate while I was there, show with the mother, who handled him at all times with perfect poise, juggling the demands of motherhood with the demands of work . . . blah, blah, blah.'

So much for New Man. The report also laid some stress on my attitude to safety, appearing to accept what Rika had told him, namely that '. . . Gen's ancient model railway layout has unsafe wiring, which might result in electric shocks or even a fire, dangers which the father does not seem able to appreciate or anticipate.'

He recommended custody to the mother. I love my boy, and couldn't easily accept that children pretty much go automatically with the mothers, so we had a court hearing to contest the matter, throughout which he referred to him as 'Jen'.

If I ever see him crossing the road in front of my car, I fear I may hesitate fatally between brake and accelerator.

Epilogue

A couple of years on, and my ties with the City have not been completely cut. My bread and butter comes from translating Japanese stock market research into English, which may be even less uplifting than the job I used to do as a sycophantic but somewhat ineffectual salesman. Occasionally, news reaches me on the wind of my various ex-colleagues, and the broking companies I used to work for.

Of these five companies, I enjoyed Merrill Lynch the most (or disliked it the least) because I found the people more interesting. I put this down to an equivalent of the Frontier Spirit, in other words, if you were prepared to work there, you were willing to take personal risks in order to have a more exciting life. Failure to perform meant being hanged from the nearest tree, which is what happened to me; success meant riches beyond the dreams of avarice, which is what happened to Alick, Henry and Charlie, and I gather that Giussi is doing quite well now too.

Michael Lewis in *Liar's Poker* refers to the satisfaction of big wages coming from there being a method of keeping score. Because I never quite got into the financial stratosphere, my opinion may be worthless, but I am sure that this theory is wrong. The satisfaction of big wages comes from the satisfaction of big wages. It's that Georgian Rectory beckoning. Most people are rather embarrassed about the score, and keep quiet about it. When, for example, the newspapers reported that Baring Securities' Christopher Heath earned over two million pounds a year and was the highest paid executive in Britain, he quickly had the method of payment changed so that this kind of publicity would never occur again, and that most private of things would remain private – the size of his wad.

We all envied Christopher Heath his two million pounds a year, but people who worked with him say that what really motivated him was the exhilaration he got out of broking. If you were to ask him directly what motivated him, he might candidly admit 'money', but possibly he would not be being as candid as he seemed. By all accounts he loved his job, and that is far more worthy of envy than the money. He once gave a friend a beautiful leather-bound diary with some extinct company's logo on it. 'That cost me £10,000,' he said, meaning that he had invested that sum in whatever the extinct project was, and all he'd got out of it was the diary. It could just be that he is one of the exceptional people who conform to Michael Lewis's theory.

Alick always used to say to me that one day he would throw it all in and retire to his Rectory, which I imagine he is well on his way to acquiring, although first he will have to have earned enough to buy the apartment in Courchevel, and put down funds to pay for his four children to be educated privately.

I am told that he continues to rub the Merrill Lynch analysts up the wrong way, which might be a mistake, because as a group, they were certainly a cut above those at Phillips and Drew. I doubt that it is Alick on his own who has driven more than half of them to leave since I left, but a living example of how bad management is in stockbroking firms. Why people trust brokers who devote their professional lives to identifying and rewarding well-managed companies with higher share prices remains beyond me.

There is a nice theory which has people in any kind of organisation being promoted to their level of incompetence. Alick is perilously close to it. He is a cracking salesman, but needs to steer clear of the casebook talented broker's mistake of getting into management (which, as observed already, doesn't exist in broking firms). He can just about handle the four or five salesmen in his immediate vicinity, but needs to limit it to that. He has gone as far as he can go without getting out of his depth. Attempts at involvement in management would be a mistake for him, because they would distract him from what he is good at, namely earning commission.

He accepted an invitation to come skiing with me, then was involved in having me fired only a few days later, which whilst not actually wrong (indeed commercially very sound), was an example of the temporary suspensions of decency which occur when you are earning too much money. I would be superhuman if I did not bear the slightest grudge, and because I believe in honesty in all things, I confess to just the smallest one.

To be completely fair to him, things were more or less out of his control. To a large extent the decision to sack me was taken by his boss, but where I feel he fell down, given that he was acting like a friend in accepting skiing invitations, was in not tipping me off. That would have been the decent thing to do. He says he didn't want to ruin my holiday, which was thoughtful, because it would have ruined the holiday, no question. But as I was about to enjoy an enforced rest of some duration, I think I would have recovered.

The extra few days of warning would have enabled me to create a game plan for survival at Merrill Lynch, or failing that, for getting a more disgracefully large pay-off out of them (getting money off Merrill Lynch is morally very sound). From Alick's point of view, he would have bought my loyalty forever. As it has turned out, the failure to do so hasn't mattered to him at all, but he wasn't to know that I would turn my back on the City.

Alick would be the first to admit that he is not the most intellectually gifted of people in the world, which may be why he is such a fine salesman. It helps not to have the mind over cluttered with other thoughts and knowledge. But selling is a young man's job in the City, and in not too many years he will be forty, ten years older than most of his clients, with whom he will have less and less in common, and his star will begin to fade. Large numbers of City people have reached the summit of their competence prematurely because of the easy times in the 1980s, and will face similar life crises soon.

I suppose I should be grateful to Alick and Merrill Lynch for forcing choices upon me that I would probably not have had the courage to make on my own. I may be in the vanguard of a new kind of worker, the army of the self-employed. Lifetime employment is long gone in the West, and under severe threat even in Japan. The shift towards short-term contracts makes excellent sense from an employer's point of view, because it gives such great flexibility, and shows signs of becoming the norm. When business is bad, it is cheap and quick to let a few people go.

What is less well understood, as more and more people get thrown on the scrapheap, is that it can suit the employee too. Having freedoms such as taking holidays when you want, living where you want, is not such a bad trade-off for being paid less and having less stability and security. If what looks like an inexorable social trend continues – a revolution even, aided by advances in telecommunications allowing you to live and work where you want – then society as a whole will become better adapted to handle the self-employed, and the self-employed themselves will become better at handling the ups and downs of what they do. Self-employment may mean a slightly duller attitude to life, with a culture of saving money, instead of spending it, so that an enforced period of no work can be taken in the stride.

It does grieve me a little to think that if self-employment becomes the norm rather than the exception, it will cause further expansion in the financial service industry, with private pension fund management taking off, and insurers offering policies to maintain income during downturns. I'm bothered because it is little understood the extent to which the profit margins on these products are hidden in the depths of computer programmes, where they are almost impossible to identify. Generally, you won't find out from the newspapers either, partly because few financial journalists have a proper understanding of what goes on, and partly because the financial pages take all their advertising from financial institutions.

Henry from Merrill Lynch once remarked to me that I am lucky. 'Jim, you can speak Japanese, you'll always have something to do. All I know is broking. I'm thirty-seven, I've got no qualifications, I'd be stuck if I lost this.'

In a fast changing world, it is probable that in due course he will lose 'that'. And then I won't feel sorry for him, because he, and Alick, are both affable, very competent people, and once the choice is forced upon them, they will find other outlets for their energies and talents, and after overcoming a period of self-doubt, no doubt stressful, do very well at whatever it is they discover to be suited to them.

(Henry is wrong about my Japanese. I learnt it when few others were bothering. I was in a programme of forty teachers sent to Japan by the British Council and Japanese Education Ministry. The same programme now sends 300 a year. I can still get away with a fairly ropey standard which would never be tolerated in a translator of French, because I am a rarity. But there are more and more people like Gen coming of age, truly bilingual, who will do my job more cheaply, more quickly, more accurately than me. I am not confident of still being a rarity in even five years' time.)

The period of transition away from full-time work is tough, though, because you can have no idea where you will emerge. I now have three jobs, all freelance. One is writing books, another is writing newspaper articles, and my bedrock income, which I don't enjoy earning, is from translating Japanese. It took a good two years to move beyond the 'Annual income twenty pounds, annual expenditure nineteen-six, result happiness. Annual income twenty pounds, annual expenditure twenty pounds ought and six, result misery,' of Mr Micawber. I had two years of misery, and I still haven't quite sussed out how to juggle the three jobs so that I don't get busy with all three simultaneously, and end up pissing off all the people who are good enough to send me work.

The period of transition probably takes at least two years. After all, a business plan for most new companies, even with the professional advice of accountants, lawyers, venture capitalists and management consultants, would not anticipate moving into profit for at least that sort of time, and anyone contemplating setting up alone needs to anticipate several years of apparent failure, combined with a significant risk of actual failure at the end of it.

I am still dogged by uncertainty, and that is stressful. I have no idea where I will be, and what I will have settled into, in three years' time, or even if I will have settled into something. But with the benefit of hindsight, I, in common with most others, can see that I have never had any idea of these things, and shouldn't be surprised if I still don't. The stress that arises from uncertainty is A Good Thing. It would be ghastly to have life perfectly mapped out, and not occasionally be swamped by surprises (sometimes they are pleasant), although one should avoid the extraneous stress arising from going through a divorce, say, or being Bosnian.

Taking risks, encountering stress, then regretting nothing when it all goes wrong is good for you, not in a masochistic hair-shirted sort of way, but truly, madly, deeply. I had no idea what I was letting myself in for when I went to Japan (having seen a might-as-well-give-it-a-go ad in the University careers room), originally for one year, eventually staying for three. I took a risk marrying my pregnant Japanese girlfriend. Gen is the delightful result. I took a risk joining Merrill Lynch. That has forced me into positive decisions.

It is much better to regret doing something, than to regret not doing something. If there are any doubts, go for it. *Je ne regrette rien* (apart from not taking out redundancy insurance).

While Alick and Henry may well have got as high as they are going in broking, and within ten years they will probably be too old for what they do, Charlie is a good deal younger, in his mid-twenties. Since I left, his business has apparently picked up. His clients have been bored into submission by his relentless monologues on market minutiae. He is young, energetic, hard working, takes no shit from anyone, and should be running his own company (making widgets or whatever). He'd be very good at it, and I would certainly invest if I knew he were in charge. I don't suppose he ever will. He is wasted in the City; he works exceptionally hard to give advice that is neither good nor bad, just competent but unexceptional, thereby filling a need with his competent but unexceptional fund manager clients. His commission figures are excellent, and I quiver with envy when I guess at how much he earns (including bonuses £150,000 plus?).

He is a driven man. As the old man who interviewed me at Merrill's originally remarked, the best salesmen are people who have something to prove. It makes them that little bit hungry. Which is why Alick and Henry will have outgrown their jobs by the time they are forty: by that age, they will have either proved it, or realised that they don't need to.

Charlie went to a very minor public school, and would like to have the plummy accent and easy manner of Etonian Alick. This manifests itself in various ways, such as one of the acutest cases of B.R.A.N.D.S (Brand Name Dependency Syndrome) that I have ever witnessed. He is a major consumer of Hermès ties and BMWs of the kind where the optional extras – spoilers, wheel arches, leather seats, throbbing octophonic stereo – are worth more than the car itself. He is moving from the Walworth Road, near my house in downmarket Camberwell (and Labour Party HQ), to a more acceptable address in smartest Chelsea. The inside of the house will be decorated with very expensive wallpaper to recreate what he imagines the inside of the Guards Club looks like. (Why anyone should want their house to look like the inside of the Guards Club is beyond me.) He will get it slightly wrong, and Alick and Henry will snigger gently behind his back every time they go there for dinner.

He'll be a stockbroker for the foreseeable future, and *very* successful, but wasted, until he wakes up one morning and realises that his Five Year Plan to become upper class is doomed to failure. Crossing class barriers is a generational thing: if he can get his kids into Eton, then the wealth he will have accumulated will mean that they will do just fine, but Charlie is inescapably, and totally identifiably, lower-middle-class. And why be ashamed of that?

Giussi is apparently doing very well. She continues to prove that it is not what you know, but who you know and what you look like. If she wants to become really mega in sales, though, I think she should abandon all those piffling European clients, even if they are friends of her Dad's, dye her hair blonde, and start selling to the Arabs.

Henry recently went through a mid-life crisis which saw him leave Merrill Lynch for a new Emerging Markets set-up at Bankers Trust. He used his company plastic to buy me a very pleasant lunch, at which he admitted that leaving had been one of the biggest mistakes of his life, and that he was miserable. Quite what he gets paid he wouldn't tell me (but I guess at £80,000 before a promised bonus he explained would not arrive because of the complete lack of business). The problem was that Bonkers Thrust had no research in the area, so Henry was finding himself sitting in the office with virtually no stock recommendations to work with, too bored and demoralised even to do the *Daily Telegraph* crossword, the only thing to look forward to being taking his friends out to lunch with the company credit card.

He'd been feeling unsatisfied and jaded at Merrill's, and decided that he needed a change of environment. The grass isn't always greener on the other side.

I had done a similar thing in leaving UBS Phillips and Drew. It had been either up or out, so I went up to Merrill Lynch, and then out of it. I think I must have had a sort of subconscious death wish, because I ought to have known enough about myself to know that I was not going to thrive at bottom line-driven Merrill's. Still, in relative terms I enjoyed it while I was there, meaning that I hated it, but less than my years at P & D, which were some of the most miserable of my life. Impersonal broking by the Henry Ford method, a bums-on-seats operation. Under the stewardship of UBS, the bums have become pretty much interchangeable – my seat was filled within a month of my departure – and a very high staff turnover rate is testimony to that.

From what one can ascertain, UBS Phillips and Drew remains as grey as ever, complete with its exciting new name, UBS Ltd. I don't think that the grey corporate Swatches that I used to give to my clients can have been the real thing because the one I nicked broke after a year, whereas the rather vulgar one I bought with my own money five years ago is working perfectly. I am very pleased with the Swiss Army knife, though.

A Mr Smith was briefly head of research there. He published a book highlighting how companies can dress up their accounts. None of the information contained in the book was very startling, certainly not to accountants or stock market analysts. P & D's corporate clients got upset at the somewhat direct way in which the information was presented, and so P & D, with typical ineptitude, tried to stop publication of the book, which hitherto had had their blessing, not to say their logo on its cover. Mr Smith went ahead, P & D issued a writ to stop publication, Mr Smith was sacked. The publicity that this gave to the book meant that a dull accounting book which might have sunk without trace became a bestseller. I hope P & D sue me.

The next bit of ineptitude was in the promotion of an oil stock analyst to be the new head of research, one Mr Beck. One wonders why Mr Beck accepted the post, because he must have known that he was on the point of resigning to join Paribas only ten days later, leaving P & D's research department running around like a headless chicken. Mr Sants, who had been head of the equities division for some years, bravely stepped in to take control of the chicken directly. Given that management in the City barely exists, while Mr Sants was doubling his duties one wonders what extra he fancied he could bring to the party. After all, the double of very little is still very little.

It is certain, though, that Limited UBS are committed to the long term. Not fly by nights, not here today gone tomorrow, like my first three employers Lawrence Prust, Vickers da Costa and Scrimgeour Kemp Gee, or like Morgan Grenfell Securities. Or here today, gone tomorrow, back again the next day, like Credit Suisse Securities, or W.I. Carc which at intervals lose all their key staff, then have to rebuild with new people again. A process now also occurring at Baring Securities, from where Christopher Heath has been promoted, er, sideways, and the majority of the rest of the key staff have fled like rats from a sinking ship.

Limited UBS's commitment to the long term is strengthened by their recent purchase of the sumptuous office building they occupy in Broadgate. When the developer of the Broadgate development went belly up, UBS was stuck with the loans it had made to get the prestigious development going. This got them some cheap office in the City's most prestigious new development. It was never UBS's intention to end up owning the space however, but being lumbered with it, it is better to run a crumby broker in it than vacate it. One can assert with no irony whatsoever that the former P & D is genuinely committed to the long term.

As observed before, it is useful for the Swiss Banks to have loss leaders because of the potential embarrassment at the amount of money which becomes theirs on the fifty year rule whereby unclaimed deposits become the property of the bank. I refer mainly to Jewish money, then money purloined by the Nazis (1940 to 1945 + 50 years = 1990 to 1995).

1991 was not, on paper, a great year for me. In it, I lost my job and then my wife. To lose one's job, Mr Parton, may be regarded as a misfortune; to lose the wife as well looks like carelessness.

The sad truth is that ninety per cent of people do not enjoy their jobs, and yet when they lose them, they are cast into misery. To a man, at least, a job is like a woman. Can't do without one, can't do with one.

Fortunately, the proportion who do not like their spouses is considerably smaller than the proportion who do not like their jobs. If we accept statistics that one in three marriages will end in divorce, then we must also accept that two in three won't, which is quite encouraging.

For the ninety per cent dropping out of work and sailing around the world is only a temporary solution. Being one of the idle and rich is a solution open to very few, but probably no solution either. Too boring. If I were to win the pools, and do what the poster suggests – sit on a beach for the rest of my life – I'd go (more) barmy in about three seconds flat. The incidence of people who die in their early sixties, shortly after starting a looked-forward-to retirement is startling. Boredom kills. You need a job, or failing that, several very absorbing hobbies.

I have found myself fulfilling many people's definition of freedom. I can stay in bed all day if I want. Or go away on holiday. Nobody can tell me what to do. I am my own master.

But this is not true freedom. The problem starts with finding the discipline to apply oneself to the job in hand. I am a bit idle, and thus arguably not well suited to self-employment.

But I love it, and won't give it up.

Wild horses wouldn't drag me screaming back into the City. (Two hundred and fifty grand might, for a short time, just until I had cleared my immediate debts.) Fortunately, after a while the problem of self-discipline becomes self-adjusting. Lying in bed too late and achieving nothing leads to monstrous self-loathing, and this forces me out of bed. It would be a bore to go through life loathing myself, I have to live with me, so staggeringly, I am often up well before eight, and not just on the days when Gen is staying and comes early into the bedroom to bounce on my head.

The solution to the problem of application works by a similar mechanism to the one whereby alcohol intake is moderated. Health and financial fears play some part, but the most immediate incentive not to drink to excess is that you have to live with yourself afterwards.

It is a depressing thought that so many people don't get satisfaction out of what they do, given that work dominates life. *Metro, boulot, dodo*, as Parisians say. (Underground, work, sleep.) What a waste of the only life you have.

'Please, God, can I have another one?'

A bored peal of thunder, more a fart actually, because He gets this request all the time. 'No mate, that's yer lot.'

Since work is pretty much unavoidable (pace the Department of Social Security), the real definition of freedom and fulfilment, of being successful at life, is loving your job. Most City people tolerate their job, regarding it as a stepping stone to that Georgian Rectory, but there is always a tiny minority who eat, sleep and breathe markets. Perhaps for them, the sums they earn are genuinely of secondary importance, a means of keeping score. They just happen to be incredibly lucky that the job they love also happens to be supremely well paid. In terms of motivation, they are little different from the obsessed computer hacker, who for no money at all devotes his life to breaking into the information systems of the Pentagon, and then doesn't even sell the information he gets, the satisfaction coming from getting it in the first place.

At this end of the scale is the man who is to be envied just as much as Christopher Heath, namely the man who earns a pittance, making his hobby his job. If not a computer hacker, perhaps an antique clock restorer, who doesn't care about money because he just loves restoring clocks. His wife is just as likely to leave him as the wife of the pressure cooker stockbroker, though. 'All you are interested in, darling, is clocks,' she says, before going off to have a steamy affair with the vicar.

Reculer pour mieux sauter. Step back to take a leap forward. When I was made redundant, I certainly lost sleep rehearsing speeches and strategies which might have saved me my job, what the French call *esprits d'escalier*, that brilliant sharp word which you should have said, but only think of as you are descending the staircase having been booted out of the mistress's bedroom. Losing my job, though, was A Good Thing.

The matrimonial break down which went with it could never be described as A Good Thing. It is all *reculer*, without any *mieux sauter-ing* at all. Well, at least not so far. I am still looking for the mother of my next five children (sod the cost, I want lots). If there was anything positive in the experience at all, it was dispensing with my worthy lawyers to conduct my own litigation in person, and having fun at the expense of Rika's solicitor, who I discovered early on had No Sense of Humour Whatsoever. I would get (acute) pleasure from winding her up, which was pathetically easy to do.

An example: I wrote this personage a long letter about something quite serious and important, but for fun inserted the words '. . . given that your record in responding to correspondence quickly is distinctly patchy . . .' I got an almost instant response, completely ignoring the serious and important points.

OSBORNES SOLICITORS
93 Parkway
London
NW1 7PP

9th November 1992

Dear Mr Parton,

We do not consider that our track record in answering correspondence quickly is patchy. We received your fax of the 9th November at 14.50 pm. You will therefore see from the time shown at the top of this fax that it is possible for us to respond quickly by fax.

Yours faithfully,

Osbornes

When the solicitor was cross with me, she would sign Osbornes, otherwise she would sign them with her name, Philippa Pearson, or when things were going really well, even Philippa.

A short time after this one, I got the following.

OSBORNES SOLICITORS
93 Parkway
London
NW1 7PP

9th November 1992

Dear Mr Parton,

Further to my fax of 20 minutes ago, you will note that the time recorded on our fax machine is one hour in advance as we have not yet changed the timing since the clocks went back. Therefore it was transmitted at 15.21 and not 16.21 as stated on the time record at the top of our paper. We are arranging for the fax clock to be put an hour back later this afternoon.

Yours faithfully,

Osbornes

In fact, she had read the time slightly wrongly.

Dunroamin' Villas
Camberwell

Philippa Pearson, esq.,
OSBORNES SOLICITORS
93 Parkway
London
NW1 7PP

9th November 1992

Dear Philippa,

Thank you for your two faxes of 9th November.

I utterly reject the suggestion that your first fax was transmitted at 15.21. It is quite clear from your letter that it was sent at 15.22.

Furthermore, it should be pointed out that I too did not change the timing on my fax when the clocks went back. My fax was thus transmitted at 13.50 not 14.50 as stated on the time record at the top of my paper.

I would therefore like to give notice that the time given on all my faxes will be one hour in advance until next summer. You will of course note that on faxes received between the hours of midnight and 1 a.m. GMT, the date will also be wrong.

Yours sincerely,

Jim Parton

I suppose I can be accused of mindless violence, but there are a couple of serious points to be extracted from this correspondence, neither of them to do with the time the faxes were sent. One is that the lawyer in question does this sort of thing on taxpayers' money, through the Legal Aid Board, and ultimately mine or Rika's, because the Legal Aid Board, if money is available, has to be paid back. Matrimonial misery is subsidised by the government.

The second is that whilst I, through my change in career, have the leisure available to write silly letters, a highly qualified professional person really ought to be above that sort of thing. I have even had letters on the subject of feeding Gen bananas in the car.

I bet Philippa Pearson hates her job. I always sensed when I talked to her (after a while she refused to take my calls) that deep down – quite a long way, admittedly – there was a thoroughly decent person trying to get out. A bit like Alick. Waiting outside some courtroom, she'd occasionally say something which had me laughing with her, not at her, but the adversarial system was bigger than she; having gone through a very demanding training, she spent her life drafting letters about bananas. All sense of perspective seemed to die when she was doing her job.

And that, roughly, is where the story ends, or rather, I hope, starts.

I have thrown off the shackles of broking for good. I now have a rather pretentious business card which says 'Jim Parton, Writer' on it. This, I find, goes down better than 'Financial Consultant, European Equity Sales'.

As a newly single man I get invited to dinner by Rory's Mum to make up the numbers from time to time.

'What do you do?'

It used to be fun to reply 'I am redundant', and watch the awkward pause, before adding that, no, I was the only one, and the reason was that I was no good at my job. But as discomfiting dinner party gambit, it has lost its force. Everybody knows somebody who is redundant.

Apart from the fact that Rory's Mum is usually trying to pair me off with one of her unmarried thirty-something-ish girlfriends, she also likes to have a 'writer' at her dinner table.

'What do you do?'

'I am a writer.'

'Do you have a set routine, getting to your word processor at nine each morning?' I wonder how many times I have been asked that, followed by, 'Can I help you write the sexy bits?'

Or, 'What do you do?'

'Self-employed, or rather self-unemployed, ha, ha, ha.' I've got bored with that one.

'Translator.' I've found that this propels the conversation on to other topics quite quickly. It seems to excite people as much as 'chartered accountant'.

Dinner party conversation inevitably revolves around the recession, increasingly global. I chip in with my bit about even the Japanese having one, quite likely worse than ours. Rory's Mum seems to find the idea of the Japanese getting their come-uppance comforting. They are the only non-white racial grouping about which the politically correct make shamelessly racist remarks. Rory's Mum couldn't quite bring herself to describe the thief of my stockbroker mobile as black. She stopped short with 'Well-built fellow, wearing a green sweatshirt'. But she does not blanche at talking about the 'Yellow peril taking over our industry'. Everyone round the dinner table nods in agreement. No matter that Gen is half Nip, and plays with Rory. And that I used to be married to a whole Nip.

The whole Nip, Rika, and I rarely talk to each other these days, which is a pity. I have little idea what she is up to therefore, except to say that it is nearly impossible to get through to her on the telephone, although the odd fax does. Most of our communications are conducted through the good offices of Miss Pearson, and her very capable – except when it comes to spelling – secretary.

Mr Gibbon continues to have a gruff exterior, but cups of tea and kindness through my troubles have meant a lot to me. He's a thoroughly decent bloke. He even complimented me on my piano playing once recently. It was a slightly double-edged compliment, delivered with the suggestion that perhaps I might have the piano tuned, but nonetheless he was acknowledging some progress.

I have taken to learning the piano by the Space Invaders method. After three mistakes I consider myself dead, and start again. My record for the 'Minute Waltz' is bar sixteen, out of 116 bars (not including repeats). In Debussy's 'First Arabesque', I always get stuck at that tinkly downwards bit (bars six and eight), to which Richard Claydermann adds such charmingly lilting syncopation. My version is syncopated because I haven't yet mastered three time in the right hand at the same time as four time in the left. Poor old Mr Gibbon.

Life has taken a turn for the worse for him. Having concreted in his garden, to make it hosable by his second wife's incontinent poodles, he had been doing some major civil engineering on a series of poodle powdering bays. This was welcome, on the reasoning that before long his entire garden would be built up, and the poodles would have the run of a centrally heated indoor set-up along the lines of the rhino pen at Regent's Park Zoo.

Unfortunately, we live in a conservation area. Although Mr Gibbon's flats are vulgar Thirties, the surrounding property is Georgian. An interfering neighbour opposite, foolishly unable to recognise the obvious benefits to the local community of Mr and Mrs Gibbons' bestiary moving indoors, had written a letter to Southwark Council. A planning officer came round, and work has been halted, pending An Inquiry.

The interfering planning officer was obviously on the side of the interfering neighbour opposite, and was trying to enlist my support, by seeing whether I would complain about the construction going on in the garden. I suggested to the planning officer that Mr Gibbon might be allowed to add a few porticos and colonnades. He could have neo-Georgian poodle parlours. You can get lovely fibreglass columns from any decent DIY outlet.

I dug out a reference book, showing Madame de Pompadour (wrong country, nearly the right era) cavorting with poodle. 'Hear, look, see, poodles are Georgian,' I tried to argue with him. But the bloke opposite is insistent that work stops and the integrity of our Georgian enclave in Camberwell is preserved. Another man with too much leisure, one has to suspect. 'That man is hima,' Rika would have said. When she says this of someone, her upper lip is definitely curled. 'Hima' is the Japanese word for leisure, free time. People with too much of it fuss about their neighbours, or build train sets, because they have nothing else to do. Mr Gibbon and I are both 'hima'. I rather like it, but if nothing else, Rika did teach me to mind my own business.

1991. Not a great year for me. I am often asked whether the marriage broke up for cultural reasons, and I don't think so. We were just different people with different interests, different friends.

Losing my job probably precipitated the break-up, but it would no doubt have happened anyway. If something is inevitable, it is probably better that it occurs sooner rather than later, so that the adjustment begins early.

I can scarcely invite sympathy about losing my job either. I went to Merrill Lynch with my eyes open. I knew they were bastards before I joined up. Also, it was not as if I wasn't being adequately compensated for the known risk.

I met a very nice Japanese girl who was left by her English husband, then shortly afterwards lost her job, a situation the mirror image of my own. She was angry at the time, she said, but she doesn't mind now. Then she went on to say something which I thought was rather profound, and a good motto along the lines of *nils illigitimae carborundum*, (pig Latin for don't let the bastards grind you down).

She said she was happy. 'Being happy is the best revenge.'

Epilogue to the epilogue 2009

The original *Bucks Stop Here* was, although we didn't use the expression at the time, about the last big credit crunch. The Japanese one. Although Japanese banks are in good shape again, so far the Japanese bear market has lasted nearly two decades.

I write this having just listened to a Radio 4 interview with Gordon Brown, formerly Chancellor of the Exchequer, by BBC economics correspondent Evan Davis. Evan was grilling away, while admitting that he had not seen the credit crunch coming, which allowed Gordon a nice let out. How could he have foreseen the replacement of boom by bust? In any case it was all the Americans' fault, added Gordon.

But lots of people foresaw it. I foresaw it for one, and most old Japan hands that I know did too, as did far more people in the City and Wall Street than are letting on.

This is one smug git writing here. I sold my cottage next to Mr Gibbon's in August 2007, the very top month for London property prices. With the proceeds I paid off the mortgage and bought a palace in Poland, in a lovely spot on the Silesian side of the Sudety Mountains. We have acres, a swimming pool, a private skating rink, an indoor tennis court, staff, a Bentley... and enough money left over to make a go of it. I feel like a banker who's pocketed his final bonus, then run for the hills.

At the time, the exchange rate for three-bed semis in Camberwell against fifty-room palaces in Silesia was about four to one. Although I had not worked in financial services for the best part of two decades, the old broker in me felt this was a valuation anomaly. This is now adjusting nicely, and the ratio looks to have headed down past two to one, and, what with the plunging pound, I reckon parity is a possibility. One three-bed in Camberwell to one fifty-room Silesian former bishop's palace; that would still seem to leave Silesian palaces undervalued, but I'm not a greedy man. If the valuation adjustment ends at two to one, I'd consider that I'd had a good war.

Meanwhile, for the sake of honesty, and because it's a convention of autobiographical humorous books that they be self-deprecating, I should qualify this smugness a little; the palace is a semi-derelict, but fascinating, project. The word 'palace' is over-egging it somewhat, but it's the one they use round here, so I'll go for that. My new wife and I occupy three of the fifty rooms, slumming it with our four toddlers, the 1984 Bentley was a rush of blood to the head which spends most of its time being fixed, the indoor tennis court is still a barn, the swimming pool is a pond, the skating rink the same pond. Nice pond though, fed by springs. We took a big risk, we're happy; so far it's working. The key word is 'risk'. Our palatial lifestyle arises not from risking a bank's money, but our own.

Mr Gibbon himself would have loved the credit crunch. Capitalism's come-uppance. We had become quite good friends by the time of his death a few years ago and he even left me £1,000 in his will. He was lonely after his wife died and I used to go round and chat to him about Beethoven. He even grew to like my piano playing, not because it got better – which it did, a little – but because the sound made him less lonely. We'd also talk about his quite distinguished career as a trade union agitator so left-wing he was expelled from the 1950s Labour party. That means very left-wing – apart from flying the red flag on St. Pancras Town Hall in 1956 when he was chairman, he suggested that the Queen move out to make rooms in Buckingham Palace available to those still homeless from World War II. He once spent six months in Brixton Gaol for assaulting a policeman on a march. The policeman had been rough-handling a female demonstrator and he intervened; that was his version, and I believe him.

His politics owed too much to Marx and Engels for current tastes, but he can hardly be blamed. His father took ten years to die from his First World War wounds, so he was unable to afford the school uniform that would have enabled him to take up the scholarship he'd won to a grammar school.

I didn't agree with his politics, but had my background not been a cosy public school one but more like his I might well have been a communist. He was a man of principle and honesty. Unlike many communists he rejected Stalin; he ran a letter-writing campaign to get Soviet dissidents out of the gulag, including the well-known Oleg Gordievsky. Communist leaves £1,000 to unrepentant capitalist in his will. It's a wonderful world.

He was permanently in despair that his son, a state school music teacher always short of cash, would do things like increase the mortgage to take his family on holiday to South Africa. 'Some day he'll have to pay it back,' he'd say. I would nod in prudent agreement, keeping the guilty secret of my own liar mortgage to myself.

When I was remortgaging for one of those low introductory teaser rates, I pointed out to the independent financial advisor that my income really didn't justify the amount I wanted to borrow.

'Just fill in any amount,' he said.

'But isn't that fraud?'

'Well, who's ripping off whom? You want the money, the bank wants to lend it, house prices are going up, everyone's a winner.'

In a way this was true; with the help of lodgers in spare rooms I never missed a mortgage payment, I was a great credit risk. Besides, if it ever looked like I might miss a mortgage payment, I could always 'release equity' and up the mortgage. Use the mortgage to pay the mortgage; I knew this was wrong, and I knew that if everyone was doing it – as they plainly were – sooner or later there would be a big pay-back day. It was just a matter of when; that's the difficult part in all economic prognostication. Just like there had been in Japan, where exactly the same mechanisms had been in play in the run up to their credit crunch.

So Mr Gibbon, who died in 2003, in seeing how his son would borrow money, probably saw it coming. Before I make myself sound too cleverly prescient, my own dinner party chat had been peppered with 'It can't go on' sort of talk from about 2003. If I'd still been an equities salesman this would have been disastrous. I would have lost all my clients for the crime of being completely and catastrophically wrong for four years. And if I'd acted on my beliefs and sold the house next to Mr Gibbon in 2003, I'd have missed out on its value doubling. It will be interesting to see if it goes back to the 2003 value. I expect it will.

So let's get back to fashionable self-deprecation and away from smugness. The Polish palace deal was a fluke, the 'when' part entirely to do with having got my Polish girlfriend pregnant, married her, got her pregnant again – and then a third time with twins. At the time of writing we have four children, the oldest of whom is still not four.

Pregnancy no. 2 was what made the timing perfect, it delayed our palace purchase, and hence, our cottage sale by twelve months or so.

[Stop press! The zloty is in freefall, even against the pound. I'm poor again. But, reader, believe me, I don't mind, I'm having fun.]

The move to Poland was to do with having not enough income to sustain a London lifestyle. Although I am not the envious type, it wasn't always easy to watch former not-especially-talented colleagues streaking off into the financial stratosphere.

Anyone, like me, who was once close to having incontinently large amounts of money, falls to philosophising about it when the money says 'goodbye'. I think the worst thing about not having loadsamoney is that it makes you mean and ungenerous, being slow with a round of drinks, that sort of thing. There is no question that having lots makes you happier and more relaxed, though there must be a ceiling beyond which it becomes meaningless; unless you really can't live without the thought that there is a Learjet on some nearby tarmac.

I back a newspaper survey which suggested that around £5 million is the amount you need. That buys several very comfortable houses, funds children though expensive schools, and so on. Too many houses, and you never have time to visit the one in St. Kitts, or the beachfront palazzo in Tuscany, or the 10 bed chalet in Klosters, and you spend most of your time worrying that the butler in each is ripping you off. And if you are lucky enough to have several honest, efficient butlers, the chances are that someone richer than you (there's always someone) will poach him.

The irony of the big bonus culture was that it didn't really make people richer. It just meant that the Tuscan palazzo ended up costing twice as much to buy. The £5 million I mentioned was from a 2003 survey. By 2007 no doubt you needed £10 million if not £15 million to retire feeling stupidly well-off.

It amuses me that I live in a Silesian schloss and achieved it all without ever having had to go through the sapping grind of being a hedge fund manager or a corporate financier, or having had to hang onto my previous career as a smile and dial equity salesman.

In London, I could see that having got into the family way again, things were going to be a struggle. In some ways the move was a fluke; but I think I should be cut some slack and allowed a little smugness. In 1991 I lost my career, then shortly afterwards my wife walked out on me. It wasn't a nice time. The divorce was messy, and for about five years she banned our teenage son Gen from making contact with me. I became heavily involved in fathers' rights, and was chairman of the charity *Families Need Fathers* for five years. Not cheery stuff. I was overdue some luck.

(Gen recently re-emerged having done well at Waseda University, Tokyo and at the University of Pennsylvania. He's achieved some sort of stardom as an actor, playing a lead in a Broadway transfer of the musical *Rent* to Tokyo, and he's booked up for the next year or two. His mother has made him take her name, so if he makes it in Hollywood – his agent has big plans for him – the person to look out for is 'Gen Shin'.)

In fact, like me and Mr Gibbon, I'm fairly certain that lots of City investment bankers, hedge fund managers and stockbrokers foresaw the Great Unwinding, though I suppose few foresaw its ferocity. I think they all knew. Certainly my City friends were all in the 'It can't go on' camp. It was just that they were also in the 'we can't stop until it does' camp too, 'and would you?' A perfectly reasonable question. Then they'd add, 'and it might go on a few years yet'. Markets often overrun in either direction. I was right about houses in 2003, but wrong about the timing. That difficult, not to say impossible, 'when' part of the investor's dilemma. House prices overran for four years. Anyway, who cares? Houses are not investments, they're not instead of pension funds. They're for living in.

Nigel, my skiing friend of Twiddles and Fluff fame, did see it coming. He got himself a job at Warburgs and stuck it for another fifteen years before taking a voluntary redundancy package. He's now set up with a young wife, two children and lives on a nice sized play-farm in Kent, the kind City people (used to) retire to in their forties. He rents part of the land to Wurzel, while he fills the time shooting and so on. He's a rotten shot. I hit more clays than him when I went to stay recently, and I'd never done it before. But he has fun country squiring it about the place. Although I'm not 100% convinced the redundancy was entirely his choice, I am 100% certain that he feels lucky to have got out a year or two before it was too late, and with a decent pay-off.

Big pay-offs are less likely to be available for those losing their jobs from now on in. These people will have to learn to adjust to a different pace of life with less money, as I did in 1991. I want to reassure them that it can sometimes be quite a good thing, but more of that later.

I believe Gordon Brown when he says he didn't see it coming; the man is so wrapped up in his own mystique, and he made critical errors like allowing himself to be fawned upon by City bankers at Downing Street. It is quite likely that he is an honest man plain deluded by a self-perception of brilliance.

Self-image; the Man who Did Away with Boom and Bust.

He must be thinking he missed his chance to go down in history, the greatest chancellor and Prime Minister ever. You can almost hear him saying in a Marlon Brando growl, 'I could have been a contender...' and it is just a little sad. Only a little; he deserves the pillory in which he will be for the rest of his life as a retired politician. (All political careers end in failure. Who said that? – it's true. Unless, like Tony Blair, you dipped out at exactly the right time. He got the 'when' right. It must hurt Gordon so much to see Tony raking in $150,000 per speech, knowing that his fee will never be so high.)

Some City people acted on their knowledge and understanding of what was going on. For example, the partners of Goldman Sachs sold their firm to investors by floating it on the stock market, and the owner of Foxtons estate agents sold out to private equity investors on both sides of the Atlantic. This was brilliant but undermines a little my theory that everyone knew. These particular private equity investors clearly didn't. But then maybe it was the investors themselves who didn't know. The bankers who did the deal probably gleefully scooped up their commission, suspecting it might be one of their last.

A family member is Chief Executive of a well-known hedge fund manager. He says, 'No publicity, Jim, no one likes us at the moment,' so, as he's family, I'll break a rule and he can remain anonymous.

They saw it coming, and shorted the banks. Some commentators have blamed the short sellers of bank shares for our problems, which is ridiculous. The banks were bankrupt, what else could a responsible fund manager do when charged with protecting his clients' money? Why is long buying any more moral than short selling?

It is only honest for all concerned that shares are correctly valued. In the case of many banks, this means zero. But in addition, this particular fund had to endure two years of under-performance while they waited for the train crash to happen. That 'when' question again. No one should make the usual anti-City accusation of short-termism.

Late baby boomers like myself have only ever experienced peace and prosperity. My relative is an economic apocalyptist, and is only slightly joking when he says, 'if you are lucky enough to have cash, the thing to do is buy gold bars and bury them in the ground'.

Meanwhile, others carried on partying, knowing that the hangover was going to be a monster, but it was worth it to be part of the orgy.

Another head of a financial stock who saw it coming was Chuck Prince, CEO of Citigroup. He would have been my ultimate boss if I'd stayed at Citicorp Scrimgeour Vickers. Shortly before the awfulness of the sub-prime crisis became apparent, and on more or less the same day as I agreed a price on the sale of my Camberwell house, he said, 'When the music stops, in terms of liquidity, things will be complicated. But as long as the music is playing you have to get up and dance. We're still dancing.'

'In terms of liquidity…' is the key phrase. He knew his bank was bust and it's hard to imagine that the CEOs of banks such as Merrill Lynch and all the other investment banks that have gone to the wall (street) didn't too.

Someone who perhaps didn't see it coming was my former boss Hector Sants, who was head of European equities during my time at UBS Philips and Drew. Although he should have done; it was his job. Throughout the crisis, and as I write, he has been the Chief Executive of the Financial Services Authority (FSA), the chief regulator of the City. Gordon Brown praised the FSA (in the BBC interview I mentioned earlier) for being better than some overseas regulators. One wonders which ones. Zimbabwe? Iceland? Ukraine?

Probably, the FSA hired Hector as a poacher willing to turn gamekeeper. He took a deep pay cut relative to what the head of a division at an international investment bank could earn. He himself said that he wanted to 'Give something back…'

My opinion is more mundane. Those who can do, those who can't, regulate.

A *Financial Times* journalist has suggested that senior bankers who lead their institutions into failure without shame deserve to be shot. Though strictly speaking Hector is no longer a banker, his is, in my view, a case in point. In Voltaire's *Candide* the remark is made, 'in England it is thought good to kill an admiral from time to time to encourage the others'. This was about the execution of Admiral Byng, who had done his best in a battle against the French at Minorca in 1756, but not enough.

'Pour encourager les autres' we need more bankers shot.

I bear Hector no grudge, his ill-luck in appearing in the *The Bucks Stop Here* is solely down to the fact that he was once my boss, therefore I cannot avoid writing about him.

But he is a good symbol of systematic failure, especially as his Job Description included the public duty of protecting the public weal. As I knew him a little, it is only right that it is him I pick on, not some other City or Wall Street grotesque who I have only ever read about in the papers, such as Merrill Lynch boss John Thain who apparently spent $1,400 on a new waste bin for his New York office while all around was financial mayhem, or Bernard Madoff-with-the-money, who I had never heard of until his $50 billion fraud was revealed.

In terms of pay, Mr Sants was worth four Chancellors of the Exchequer in the year that Northern Rock failed. I'd found it odd that my own pay had been one Chancellor back when I was a broker. Four chancellors. That's a bit like one three-bed semi in Camberwell being worth four Silesian palaces. A valuation anomaly.

I have absolutely nothing against people earning obscene amounts of money, unless, as is the case of Mr Sants, or indeed of bankrupt RBS's Fred the Shred Goodwin and his £700,000 pension. These amounts were achieved with no personal risk whatsoever and included manifest failure to do the job so handsomely paid for.

I remember sitting next to crusty old partners at Lawrence Prust, the first firm I worked for. They'd describe the 1974 bear market, the time of the three day week and the miners' strikes. Business dwindled away to almost nothing, but they dipped into their own pockets and kept the firm going. In the bad times, they effectively had negative bonuses

Losing a huge bonus and large salary isn't all bad. To put this in perspective it helps to own a palace in Poland. Mine used to belong to a man called Fritz Lorenz. It is in Silesia, a part of Poland that wasn't Poland until 1945. It was Prussia from 1745 to 1945 and before that Austro-Hungary. My village was 100% German not Polish. The Germans were completely ethnically cleansed from the area inside Poland's new borders as agreed between Stalin, Churchill and Roosevelt at Teheran in 1943, place names were changed, gravestones ripped up, everything.

In 1945 Fritz lost everything. I have met his family, and there is every reason to think he was 'a good German' caught in the middle of a bad war not of his making. But in the context of 1945, not many people would have felt sorry for him.

He lost a lovely house, a huge farm, as well as ownership of a big sugar manufacturing company. In fact, his nephew told me it's thought that he managed to get a train full of sugar out of Silesia to Austria as the war ended, and being intelligent, resourceful and entrepreneurial, after the war he did OK. My point is that City people really will have to go without bonuses for a while, and that won't be too bad for them. They'll get over it, even the distress sellers of mansions in Holland Park.

If the financial services industry contracts permanently, as it's bound to, smart people will have sent their metaphorical trains of sugar off to Austria. There will be casualties, there will be lots of work for divorce lawyers, ordinary people losing their ordinary jobs will wonder what it is they did wrong, and anger will mount against those who pocketed fortunes for being not-so-talented, and risking other people's money, rather than their own.

Perhaps, as the City shrinks there is reason to be optimistic. Disproportionately it sucked in people who actually did have talent, many who worked there were entrepreneurial and highly intelligent.

These brains and this flair, these special and unique talents, will be released into the wider economy where they can do some real good. An example; a twenty-five year old lad in my rugby team, who has lost his job in property derivatives, and can't get another. He's thinking of going back into nuclear physics, his training, where he may work on the electricity industry's shortage of nuclear power stations.

In my own case, once I'd got over the hurtful fact that I was a City reject after 1991, I found lots of interesting things to do; writing books, journalism, an investment in Cubana – a theme restaurant, where the dividend has been fun rather than money (it was meant to be money). It's not a cliché to say that there are those who are time rich and cash poor, and I'd prefer to be time rich any day. Though to have both time and cash would be better still.

I've had loads more fun than would have been possible in the City. Bank of England chief Mervyn King said so many City people, 'thought that the purpose of a bonus and compensation was to give them a chance to leave the City to do something they really wanted to do... I think that's rather sad.'

He might have added that few succeeded. Too many became slaves to their bonuses. For me, being made redundant in 1991 was a lucky escape. I was Robbie William's ghost-writer for one book. Imagine the excitement of standing on the stage in front of 35,000 muddy fans at Glastonbury next to Nicky from All Saints and Robbie's mum.

I took up rugby again. I remember my first game in about 1992, aged 32, for a team called the London Japanese. Each time I got knocked over, I couldn't believe how difficult it was to stand up again. 'I'm still young, for goodness sake, what's happened to me?'

My body was a wreck from sitting in a City office all day. Pushing 50, I'm still playing, if knocked over I can get up again, and, in one of the greatest honours of my life, the Kew Occasionals RFC made me their president. I've just found a team in Poland, so I'm not finished yet. Had I carried on as an equity salesman this would never have been possible. I've also played a lot of tennis, and my piano playing is still getting better. Für Elise is a distant memory, my five-year plan is a Rachmaninov Prelude now. And with no neighbours to disturb I could play at midnight, if it wasn't minus 10 in the hall.

A lot of the City people will be confused by their early and enforced retirements and that their big-spending dream will never materialise. But they will be fine, though it will be painful for them for a period, as it was for me. For all these people, the end of the financial services industry as we know it is an opportunity which many will end up grateful for, though they may not know it now.

Must go, there's been a sharp frost, and the ice on the pond is good today.

More reviews of The Bucks Stop Here

'The former equity salesman Jim Parton writes that media punditry is "a sure sign of mediocrity". His crestfallen memoir of City broking in the early 1990s lacks all grace and gravitas. So what? As a pungent first-hand account of the "temporary suspensions of decency which occur when you are earning too much money", it has few recent rivals. As an inflammatory summer beach-read for the unwaged and underpaid, it has none.

Parton's scandal strewn narrative shows one way to demysitfy the Square Mile's secrets. He adopts the larky, laddish voice beloved of all publishers these days. Since it might just help him to reach the first-time investor in unit trusts (70 per cent of which fall short of the index for their sector) this blokery can be forgiven.'

Boyd Tonkin
New Statesman and Society, 8th July 1994

'City insiders will find this book compelling, but it should be required reading for all those, inside or outside the City, who have ever harboured the faintest, niggling suspicion that they are not worth their pay cheque.

He is as honest about his own shortcomings as he is about others. His boss thought he was 'crap', and he thought his boss was a 'nasty bastard'.

Parton is always economical in his character portrayals, as in the deliciously brief: 'Let's be quite honest. He is a bastard and I hate him.' The book amusingly attacks anyone and everyone who plays a role on the City stage: personnel managers, the Sloanes who haunt dealing rooms flogging men's shirts and the entire French race, to name a few.

The description of his abortive job hunt contains a wonderful indictment of headhunters. I have seen many people in Parton's shoes and his portrayal is painfully accurate.

He is delightful on the subject of responses to the standard interviewing questions, such as 'What motivates you?', to which the correct answer is: 'Lots and lots of money.'

Being honest about the City is a dangerous game. I think it will pay off for Jim Parton, but if he is really nursing any hope of being lured back with a quarter-of-a-million package, he'd be well advised to put that dream in his bottom drawer and forget all about it.

Parton is blessed with a lovely, comic turn of phrase, reminiscent of Bill Bryson, and although his publisher let the odd hideously tangled sentence through the editorial net, it didn't spoil my enjoyment.

I was more bothered by the occasional moments when his commendable cynicism lapsed into grapes of an exceedingly sour variety, but he clearly had a tough year and he deserves a break.

This is a personal testament, and towards the end of it I was asking three questions. Is he a nice chap? Almost definitely. Is he right about the City? Yes and no; I agree a lot of brokers are overpaid and arrogant, but he seems unlucky to have been surrounded by such dreadfully mediocre specimens.

Finally, is he a good writer? Yes, he is. He keeps his knife sheathed for the analysts, but I am sure he would agree with me that far too many are guilty of sitting on the fence when it comes to a recommendation, so I'll now stick my neck out: It's a Buy.'

Juliette Mead
The Daily Mail, 16th July 1994

'When Jim Parton was selling equities in for American investment bank Merrill Lynch, he would get into work at 7 am to catch the Tokyo market and stay until well into the evening. 'I got home knackered. My son was already asleep and I was monosyllabic to my wife. I went to bed at 10.30 – that was if I had not already dropped off over my supper.'

He has since 'got a life', as he puts it, by foresaking stocks and shares to spend his days writing at home in Camberwell. His engaging first book, *The Bucks Stop Here*, narrates the premature end of his City career – and of his marriage – in vivid, gossipy detail and has become a bestseller in most Square Mile bookshops.

One reason that it has struck a chord is that it illustrates a phenomenon which has only recently attracted the wider attention it deserves: chronic overwork.

Sitting in the Observer's newsroom writing this at 10 pm, it seems clear to me that, despite compelling evidence, most of us are so far paying only lip service to the pressing need to work less hard. There is a long way to go before we genuinely realise that we have got trapped in a topsy-turvy culture where too many people have no job and too many others do enough work for two...'

Lisa O'Kelly
The Observer